FUNDRAISING
FREEDOM

FUNDRAISING FREEDOM

7 STEPS TO BUILD & SUSTAIN YOUR NEXT CAMPAIGN

MARY VALLONI

AUTHOR ACADEMY elite

© 2016 by Mary Valloni

Published by Author Academy Elite
P.O. Box 43, Powell, OH 43035
www.AuthorAcademyElite.com

Printed in the United States of America

Paperback ISBN-13: 978-1-943526-89-5
Hardcover ISBN-13: 978-1-943526-88-8
Library of Congress Control Number: 2016914452

Cover Design: limitlessgraphicdesign.com
Author Photography: shariphotography.com

DEDICATION

In memory of my dad, Lawrence Lindgren, my biggest cheerleader and the most charitable person in my life.

To my husband, Geno, for pushing me daily to be a better me, to remain curious, and to never follow the rules.

To my incredible team of mentors, family, friends, and clients who were a part of making this book a reality. I am so grateful for each of you.

To all the volunteers and donors who said yes throughout the years and to those who said no for reminding me to stay the course and to never give up.

CONTENTS

FOREWORD

All nonprofit leaders need someone who can cut through the good and bad fundraising advice and provide an easy, practical way to raise funds. In *Fundraising Freedom*, Mary Valloni makes it clear that she is that someone as she guides you on the fundraiser's journey.

Don't be left to figure it out on your own. Her insight and hands-on advice ensures you won't go it alone. Mary shares her personal stories about how she has navigated the process so you know exactly what steps to take. Knowledge is only good if we implement the information and take action, and Mary pushes you to do just that.

This book is about more than just raising money. It's about relationships. It's about creating a plan where lives are intertwined and it leads you back to fulfilling your vision. Securing financial gifts is just a result when you provide value to those you serve. The 7 Steps are here so you never have to question what's next. You will know exactly what the game plan is and you'll have the freedom to make better decisions, resulting in greater impact.

This content is clear and concise, and an easy read for a new nonprofit leader, but it comes packed with content for a novice fundraiser as well. Most of us are guilty of appearing busy, but busy doesn't equal results. Mary wants you to see results, and these steps will get you there.

I've watched this book come together and I'm excited for you because I know the words on the following pages will get you on the right path to fully fund your budget. I am passionate about igniting souls and I believe this content will spark a flame and ignite something incredible in nonprofits around the globe.

Kary Oberbrunner
Author of *ELIXIR Project, Day Job to Dream Job,*
The Deeper Path, and *Your Secret Name*

INTRODUCTION

I was seven years old when I sat by and watched all my toys and clothes being boxed up and loaded into the car. We were moving. The car ride was a familiar drive as we took it often to visit my grandmother, but I had a strange new feeling when my parents, sister, and I walked through the front door of an empty two-bedroom apartment. Back then, I had no idea how that moment would forever change my life.

I was the youngest of seven children that spanned over sixteen years in age. Finances were tight, but we were never without. As a teenager I started to realize how different we lived, and I became fascinated with those who had more. My friends tended to come from wealthier homes where I could escape from my reality. My friends and their parents made sure I had everything they had. I had access to their name brand clothes, fancy vacations, meals at nice restaurants...and so for brief moments of time, I was one of them.

Many people have invested in my life, and in a sense, donated to my personal cause. I've seen generosity at its best with no strings attached, no expectations of being paid back or being recognized, just pure joy to invest in my life.

In elementary school, I caught the fundraising bug when I became the top candy bar fundraiser in my class. From the outside looking in, it appeared to my classmates that we had a small family of four. What they didn't know was that the other half of my family lived on the university campus on the opposite side of town. My dad and I would drive to campus to visit my siblings, and we'd go door to door through campus housing. Those dollar candy bars flew out of the box. My classmates didn't stand a chance.

The day I was awarded the top fundraiser in my class, something came alive in me. I began raising funds for class trips, cheerleading uniforms, school competitions, and then mission trips and charities. As soon as I realized I could raise funds to help others in need, I was hooked. I had found my calling.

Although I care deeply about charitable causes, I began to connect more and more to the individuals who gave. I could see firsthand how wealth brought its own challenges and responsibilities. It is a common misconception that money can fix all of our problems—and yes, a certain amount will make our lives slightly easier—but someone of great wealth could destroy a nonprofit if they gave more than that individual or charity could handle. I also saw the genuine interest my donors had in my own life. They wanted to invest in me because they could see that they were making a difference through me.

It's been thirty years since I received that candy bar fundraising award, and I've spent the past fifteen years as a fundraising professional raising well over $10 million for charity. Some of those dollars were painful, but every volunteer I've recruited and every dollar I've raised gave me the content for this book.

Since those candy bars, I have put on nearly every kind of fundraiser under the sun. I sold flowers, stuffed animals, wrapping paper, cookies, and popcorn. I brought in silent and live auction items, put on horse shows, car shows, and concerts. I took donations outside of grocery stores and department stores; hosted galas, walks, runs, skeet shoots, golf tournaments, telethons, online fundraisers, created social media campaigns, newsletters, and sent out direct mail. I wrote letters, grants, corporate campaigns, matching gifts, cause marketing campaigns, sponsorships—and the list goes on. It was exhausting to put on some of these fundraisers, but with each new experience I learned the valuable lessons that are included in this book.

I don't regret any of the experiences I've had, but I also know there is a much easier way and a less stressful way to fundraise. I hope to help you avoid the pitfalls and give you the tips I used to raise over $500,000 with a first-year event with an effective, empowered team. There are very few new ideas, but I believe fundraising can be way more fun with this approach. I hope to serve as your guide throughout the process and help you avoid unnecessary heartache and exhaustion as you grow to become a more experienced and focused fundraiser.

This plan isn't complicated but it does take a strong leader who is willing to make a change. It's no longer about what's in it for you, the fundraiser, but rather, what's in it for us, the team.

When I first started teaching these steps I wasn't sure the results could be replicated, but with each new organization and individual who followed the plan I saw powerful results over and over again. This is a proven plan, and I am confident that this is the plan for you and your organization if you want long-term sustainability, growth, and fundraising freedom.

I encourage you to jump in and scan through the seven proven steps below and identify where you are in the plan. The steps spell out the word FREEDOM and will be the most effective if you can put them to memory. Memorizing the steps will allow you to reflect on previous steps and plan ahead for what is to come.

Step 1: Focus Your Vision

Step 2: Run Your Research

Step 3: Enlist Your Team

Step 4: Enhance Your Brand

Step 5: Deploy Your Team

Step 6: Organize Your Ask

Step 7: Make Your Difference

You may have an established nonprofit or you may just be getting started. For those of you starting a new campaign, follow the steps in chronological order. Note that as you get into your fundraising you will jump to the appropriate step as needed. For instance, when you get to Step 4 and are creating your logo, you will reflect back to your vision (Step 1), you'll run your research (Step 2), and enlist your team's help (Step 3) as you create and choose your logo.

I am excited to get these steps into the hands of you, the reader, knowing that lives will be changed because of the work you are and will be doing. I am confident that you are about to take a journey that will forever change your thoughts around fundraising. Let's get started!

CHAPTER 1

STEP 1: FOCUS YOUR VISION

"Fake it until you make it!"

That's what I told myself last May of 2002. I was sitting in my first job interview out of college for the development director position with a national nonprofit organization. I wanted that job more than anything.

I was in a boardroom with the five most influential leaders in the organization as they asked me, a scared twenty-one-year-old, to sell them the bottle of water on the table in front of me. I think I blacked out. Needless to say, I didn't get the job, but that wasn't the end of my story. I graduated from college and took the first job offered to me, which was radio sales.

I was selling $99, fifteen-second ads with a local Christian radio station. I cried every day I went in to work. I got hung up on, yelled at, and had the door slammed in my face too many times to count. I knew this was not the right fit for me. Was I good at it? Yeah, I was great at it.

I've never been afraid of sales, but I didn't love it, and I knew that if I didn't love it, I couldn't sell it.

In an attempt to get away from the phones, I punched out for lunch and went to the city utilities building to pay my utility bill on the apartment my husband and I had just moved into. I took a number as I walked in and sat in the only seat open next to two men.

Everyone was watching the numbers as they were called, and one of the guys next to me started to make conversation. He commented about how busy they were and I responded that I was in no hurry to get back to the job I hated. He immediately started to ask questions and shared a little about himself.

He said that his wife just took a new fundraising job at a local charity. I asked a few more questions before it became apparent that she was better at selling a water bottle than I was. I quickly shared with him how happy I was for his wife, but how her new job meant that I was selling radio ads.

He gave me the number of the director and said they were hiring an administrative assistant and I should give them a call. I was so tired and broken by this point that I would have mopped their floors if they would hire me.

It was hard for me at twenty-one years of age to see that I deserved nothing. I didn't deserve the development director position and I didn't deserve a big paycheck just because I graduated from college. I knew I didn't have the experience necessary to be hired for the position, and I understood they couldn't hand me that level of responsibility, but what were the odds that I'd sit down next to the husband of the woman who got the job I wanted? It reminded me that we might not get everything we want in the way that we want it, but that doesn't mean we should give up.

CLIMB THE LADDER

When I reflect back on those days, I realize I was trying to climb the ladder—not the corporate ladder but an actual ladder. When I interviewed for that first job, I hadn't even pulled the ladder out of the closet yet, but I was so overconfident thinking I had it all figured out. I was so wrong. The 7 Steps I share in this book are here for you to use in most any circumstance, but they are much like the steps on a ladder. You may only need a step stool to reach some of your goals while others will be so big it will feel like you'll need a ladder that can extend beyond the rooftop.

I'm not a huge fan of heights, and I'd say most people afraid of heights would agree that the more steps you take on a ladder, a diving board or up a mountain, the more nerve-racking it becomes. It never fails that the higher I climb, the more butterflies show up in my stomach and fear creeps in. My mind starts running scary "what if" thoughts over and over. What if I fall? What if I slip or lose my balance? What if the ladder tips over?

Sometimes that anxiety is so debilitating and overwhelming that we never even take the first step and our dreams end before we've even begun. There are a lot of people in the world who never consider stepping foot on the ladder toward their dreams, and I don't want that to be you. Everything is achievable; we just have to break it down into easy steps and take it one at a time.

It takes a certain level of strength to climb any ladder, big or small, and it takes at least a little bit of effort to climb to the top. When I sat in that first interview, I was just getting a glimpse into what I wanted my life to look like. I was just getting started, and after I got that first rejection letter, I realized in that moment just how badly

I wanted it. I had clarity that I wanted to be a fundraiser, and I was willing to do whatever it would take to make that a reality.

No matter what it is you want, you have to have a desire to do it. Some people have dreams of being a professional athlete or a musician. They want the fame and fortune that come with it, but they don't have the desire to sacrifice for it. Whatever the vision is, you have to be willing in this moment to say to yourself that you will do whatever it takes to make it happen. If you don't have the desire, there is no need to continue on. All the remaining steps are worthless without the desire.

When I realized my vision was to be a fundraiser, my desire to make that happen became laser focused. I pictured myself in that job and I wanted it. So I went back and interviewed for the administrative assistant position and was offered the job. I took it with the intention of working my way into the development position I wanted.

Eighteen months later, the development director announced she was resigning and recommended that I be next in line. I put the work in and no one knew the job better than I did. For eighteen months, I shadowed the director and assisted her in every aspect of the job. I gained the experience I needed and I was confident that I was the best person to fill the position.

It didn't take long for me to realize that the only one stopping me from achieving my vision was myself. If I wanted to climb the ladder I had to take the first step. Your first task is to decide whether you have the desire to do this. Are you willing to take the first step on the ladder to focus your vision?

YOUR INNER THOUGHTS

When we think of children we often describe them as curious, imaginative, and without worry or a care in the world. Children have an innocence that many of us seek to protect for as long as possible and for good reason. We want them to believe in the mystery of Santa Claus, the Tooth Fairy, and the Easter Bunny. We want them to believe that they can be whatever they want to be when they grow up. We try to protect them from anyone who tries to take their joy away, and yet as we age, we don't protect ourselves from those same negative thoughts that consume and steal our joy.

We rationalize why things would never work out and we find excuses for why it would be nearly impossible for our vision to come true. No matter where you are in life, you always have two choices: positive self-talk or negative self-talk.

It is easy to get down on yourself when that's all you hear from the people around you. If your closest group of friends, family, or mentors are pumping negativity into your head, it's time to move them out of your inner circle.

This may be a family member that you can't remove from your life, but you do have a choice as to how much time and energy you give to them. Entrepreneur, author, and speaker Jim Rohn says, "You are the average of the five people you spend the most time with." This statement has been proven over and over again.

Take for instance Thomas Edison and Henry Ford. Thomas Edison, known for his inventions of electric light, power utilities, sound recording and motion pictures, and Henry Ford, the founder of the Ford Motor Company, were longtime friends. Ford worked as an engineer under Edison at the Edison Illuminating Company from 1891 to 1898. Edison is credited with giving Ford the confidence to build his own gas-powered car, while Ford advised Edison to find a substitute for rubber. They also vacationed together alongside other influential leaders of their time.[1]

Edison and Ford needed each other just like you need your team of family, friends, and mentors. Be sure you make a conscious choice as to who you will spend the most time with. The people you spend time with will influence your thoughts, and your thoughts will impact your daily decisions.

FIND YOUR WHY

Children are known for their curiosity and they love to ask why.

Why do birds fly?

Why is that man homeless?

Why do people get sick?

Why, why, why...

We all have that child in us who asks why things have to be done the way they are done.

Why do I have to eat my vegetables?

Why can't I eat ice cream for dinner?

We don't ask ourselves what, we ask *why.*

The remaining six steps will dig into the "How to" and the "What you should do," but this step helps you determine the why so you can stay focused throughout all the hard work you're going to invest in the upcoming steps.

The older we get, the more we focus on what we should do, and we forget to ask why we're even doing it in the first place. It's not good enough to respond with the answer "just because." We need to know our why.

Subconsciously, we know that we're never going to lose ten pounds, save money for retirement, take the dream vacation, etc. if we don't have the answer to the question why.

Children have no problem asking for help or asking questions, but with age comes pride. Discovering what is at the root of your pride will help you to overcome it. We ask for help all the time, we just don't always realize it. Sometimes we pay for help when we get our haircut, are served at a restaurant, or when our groceries are bagged at the grocery store.

Other times we receive help without paying for it, like when someone pays for your meal, offers to help you move, or gives you a ride to the airport. Each scenario took time, money, and resources. Everyone's time, money, and resources are valuable because we have a finite amount of it. We are all going to use it in some way or another so there is no reason to allow pride to get in the way and deter you from asking for help.

WHY SHOULD ANYONE CARE

Most people will mistakenly jump to Step 6 when they have funds to raise. They think the best thing to do is just knock on as many doors as possible and someone will eventually say yes. Sadly, that is the least effective way to fundraise.

The reality is that you may get small donations because they feel sorry for you or they don't feel the pain of giving away a few dollars, but if you want the big gifts and the gifts that are repeated, you need to know and share WHY you need their help, and be passionate about it. If you think someone is going to give you a check because you "say" you're going to cure cancer or you "say" you are going to save babies, it's just not good enough.

This is the step where you get to paint the picture for your future supporters, and you get to tell the story as if everything went perfectly and the outcomes are exactly how you envision them to be. You create the foundation so your vision becomes a reality.

Do you want to raise $500, $5,000, $50,000? $500,000? $5 million? Anything is possible, but if you set up a plan to raise $500, you'll never raise $5 million with the same plan.

I encourage you to keep a journal. The ability to envision your future is a powerful thing. Being able to verbalize what you want will allow you to put into words what you want to accomplish. This also allows you to verbalize it to others. When you write down what you want, the details will start to fill in as you visualize what you want your future to look like. As you reflect back, you will see how your daily choices and decisions are influenced by your vision.

FIND YOUR MISSION AND VISION

Having focus on your vision will allow you to determine with clarity what you are and what you are not. The best way to do this is through a mission and vision statement. During the vision step you create legitimacy. You say to yourself and to others that you're going to do it, you're going to do it well, and you're clear about the direction you're going.

If you skip over this part of Step 1, you are allowing uncertainty to creep in. You are telling your potential donors that you are disorganized and you may or may not do what you say you're going to do, because you don't even know if you are capable of doing it.

Successful organizations and businesses have both mission and vision statements that define their decisions. These will not only give you clear direction but also show your donors and constituents that you are going to do what you say you are going to do regardless of who is involved.

The mission and vision statements say a lot about who you are. This is where you establish why you exist (the mission) and your desired end state (the vision).

The mission statement should:

- Be Concise: a sentence or two that describes the reason the organization, program, or individual exists;
- Define: the present state and purpose of your organization;
- Be Used: to make decisions about priorities, actions, and responsibilities;
- Be Easy to Recite: by everyone;

- Be Unique: recognizably yours.
- Answer the Questions:
  - What do you or your organization do?
  - Who do you serve?
  - How do you serve your constituents?
  - Where do you work? (Geographic location)

Individuals inside and outside of your organization should know the mission statement and should understand your primary purpose.

The vision statement should:

- Be Concise: a sentence that describes the long-term change that will result from your work, the desired end state;
- Define: the mental picture of what you want to achieve over time;
- Be Used: to lead your group or organization to achieve results;
- Be Easy to Recite: by those involved. All members of your team can look towards the vision statement for answers regarding direction;
- Be Unique: you're not confused with your mission statement and will withstand changes to your organization's leadership and changes in the economy;
- Consider the Questions:
  - What changes are you making?
  - In a perfect world, what would your end-state look like?
  - What does success look like?

Staff and volunteers should be able to recite the vision statement with ease and understand the direction of your cause with certainty and clarity.

Here are a few samples of mission (M) and vision (V) statements to give you an idea of how to create your own.[2]

Habitat for Humanity
(M) Seeking to put God's love into action, Habitat for Humanity brings people together to build homes, communities, and hope.
(V) A world where everyone has a decent place to live.

Make-A-Wish
(M) We grant the wishes of children with life-threatening medical conditions to enrich the human experience with hope, strength, and joy.
(V) Our vision is that people everywhere will share the power of a wish.

Boy Scouts of America
(M) To prepare young people to make ethical and moral choices over their lifetimes by instilling in them the values of the Scout Oath and Law.
(V) To prepare every eligible youth in America to become a responsible, participating citizen and leader who is guided by the Scout Oath and Law.

Amnesty International
(M) To undertake research and action focused on preventing and ending grave abuses of these rights.
(V) Amnesty International's vision is of a world in which every person enjoys all of the human rights enshrined in the Universal Declaration of Human Rights and other international human rights instruments.

ASPCA
(M) That the United States is a humane community in which all animals are treated with respect and kindness. (V) To enhance quality of life for all as we age. We lead positive social change and deliver value to members through information, advocacy, and service.

By creating mission and vision statements, you are telling your entire team, including your donors, what they are supporting when they give to your cause. Take time to make this a priority before you move forward. This is the time to focus your vision and make it as clear and concise as possible so you are proud of who you are and what you stand for.

SET A TIMELINE

Now that you've started to feel like you're getting your arms wrapped around the vision, it's time to create a timeline. If you want your vision to become a reality, it is absolutely necessary that you set multiple timelines. You will want to create a 3-, 6-, and 12-month timeline as well as a long-term business plan.

Let's say one of your primary goals is to work full-time as a director or a staff member of your nonprofit organization. Your priority is to create your exit strategy and determine how quickly you want to see that happen.

Do you want to be out of your job in two weeks, three months, six months, or next year? Regardless of the timeframe, you need to set a date. If you don't set a date it will never get done. We all know how that works. We have great intentions but we don't necessarily have the desire to make the commitment.

The timeline forces you to put a date on the calendar, which gives you something to look forward to as well as give you a sense of urgency. It also creates focus when distractions inevitably come your way.

When I decided to start my business, I told my mentor I wanted to resign from my full-time job in six months. I pulled out the calendar and looked at six months from that day, and immediately searched for a commemorative date on the calendar. I encourage you to pick a date that means something to you to increase the emotion around the date.

The experience that pushed me to fulfill my business vision was the loss of my dad to cancer in 2013. I did a lot of self-evaluation the following year. My dad was sixty-nine years old, and I never anticipated he would be gone at that young of an age. His death made me realize that our years are numbered, and I couldn't push my vision off any longer. So when I looked at the calendar and saw six months from that date was the end of November, I chose my dad's birthday, November 28, as my goal date.

The date was set and everything became real. I was bringing the idea and my vision to life. I told myself, "I'm going to resign in six months." I sat in that moment and repeated the date over and over in my head. I had to believe this was my new reality.

Whenever setting a goal, I recommend using the S.M.A.R.T. goal process, which is what I did here.

Was it Specific? Yes.

Was it Measurable? Yes.

Was it Attainable? Yes.

Was it Realistic? Yes.

Was it Timely? Yes.

So I pulled out a sheet of paper and began the timeline. I wrote out the months May, June, July, August, September, October, and on the 28th of November, I put down: *RESIGN; Dad's birthday.* Under each month I had a bullet point list of what I was going to do to make sure that November 28 was my last day on the job.

Once your timeline is complete, continue to add to it and re-evaluate as needed, but this is the framework you should use to achieve your vision. If I have a goal to raise $500,000, the calendar will show that $500,000 deadline. It must be specific, measurable, attainable, realistic, and timely. Once you have that number or project goal on your timeline, it is up to you and your team to figure out how to get there. It doesn't matter what road you take as long as you get to the goal by the date on your calendar.

Without vision, you'll find yourself getting lost and distracted along the way. Create a direct path and stay on it until you get there. You'll feel like there are days that you barely move, but just stay the course and you'll see progress that will increase your desire to complete each project. The timeline is a necessity and should be unique to each project, but one that can be modified as needed.

BUILD A BUDGET

Individuals make up 71% of all donations in the United States[3], so it's important to think about how these individuals view you and your organization. Sadly, not all organizations or their leadership have been honest over the years, which has led to skepticism as to whether non-profits are worthy of donor's dollars. Donors are more cautious now than ever as to how donations are being used. It is your responsibility to create transparency through your budget.

Individuals and giving entities are becoming more interested in seeing your annual report and your financial statements. The budget is a clearly defined guide to the health of your organization. It will show how diversified you are and how you are using dollars to meet your mission and vision. A budget is necessary whether you are working on a small or big project. Every line item is important to document.

Note that Charity Navigator, Better Business Bureau, and other charity watchdog organizations will review your organization based on accountability and transparency. Keep in mind that the general guidelines of spending include 15% or less on administrative costs and 30% or less on fundraising, which allows 55% or more to cover your program expenses.[4]

Everyone wants to feel like they are making a difference. Some are happy to pay for administration and fundraising expenses because they understand that you can't function without office space, printing supplies, administrative support, and the events that help raise your funds.

Now that you have focused your vision, you know your "WHY." At this point, you should have your mission and vision statements completed and you are armed with your timeline and budget. You are now ready to move on to the next step. The following chapters will give you the "HOW TO" as you move from step to step in your journey toward fundraising freedom. Buckle up. Here we go!

CHAPTER 2

STEP 2: RUN YOUR RESEARCH

"My name is Sherlock Holmes. It is my business to know what other people don't know." – Sherlock Holmes in *The Adventures of the Blue Carbuncle*

I'd only been working a month on the job at the American Cancer Society when I was given the opportunity to meet one-on-one with the organization's Vice President of Development. My co-workers tried to prepare me for this meeting by letting me know what a big deal it was for the VP to take the time to meet with me. He was the go-to guy to train and mentor staff and volunteers across the country. He had been with the organization for over thirty years and was very well respected.

During our first meeting together, he invested a lot of wisdom and advice in me knowing that I was starting from scratch, but no single piece of advice was able to transform my thinking as much as this one had.

"Be Sherlock Holmes!"

Yes, be Sherlock Holmes! This was it. This was the secret to all the work that was to come. If I didn't know my audience, how would I ever know if they were capable of giving to my organization?

The National Institutes of Health (NIH) invests nearly $32.3 billion annually in American medical research alone.[1] Scientists are looking at environmental changes, and people are dedicating years of their lives to go to Mars in search of breakthroughs in understanding the Earth, space, and science. These are complicated issues, and people are risking their lives for answers. Some spend their entire lives researching a topic, and yet, may never find what they are looking for.

If you stick to the plan, you'll be at Step 7 before you know it, making a difference and celebrating your success. This is the most time-intensive step, and for some projects, it may take years of research, and for others, it may only take minutes, hours, or days to complete. If you want to raise a few hundred dollars on a bake sale, garage sale, or a carwash, you won't need much research, but if you want to raise thousands or hundreds of thousands, your research will increase exponentially.

During that initial meeting with the VP of Development, I was given clear direction. He said, "Take the next several months to do your Sherlock Holmes research. Find out everything you can about the events in your community. Who are the elite 15%? Where are they spending their time? Your research is critical to your success, so go do it."

During our time together, I handed him a copy of the socialite magazine from my community. On the cover was a picture of a man and a woman who I thought should be the lead volunteers for the event I was working on. He asked me, "What do you know about them?" I responded, "Well, I know they're wealthy. They're well respected, and I know they aren't involved in many large-scale events in town."

He continued to ask more questions about the couple, and honestly, I realized I didn't know very much about them. I just wanted them involved, but I hadn't done any research to know if this was even something they would consider. At the end of our conversation, I wasn't very confident that they were a good fit at all, but his parting advice was, "Get on it! Go be Sherlock Holmes, and don't assume anyone is a good fit until you've done your homework."

So that's what I did. I immersed myself in the work. I wanted this to be the top event in my community. I knew how to put on events, but I had never been able to get over the $25,000 mark. I had already had it in my head that I wanted to raise $1 million. I had access to everything I needed to be successful, and if he told me to do my research, then that's exactly what I was going to do.

I had a strong organization backing me with 96% brand recognition[2], and I had a very experienced leadership team that included a passionate group of volunteers and staff. This man was overseeing events that raised over $50 million, with his largest event raising nearly $4 million alone. I wanted to do this right, which meant I needed to take his advice and become Sherlock Holmes.

Sherlock Holmes is a fictional character but he embodies the very thing that we as fundraisers should be: detectives. Holmes had the ability to draw big conclusions from small observations. We all have the ability to draw conclusions of each other, plus we have a lot more tools than Sherlock ever had. With the addition of the Internet and social media, we can get a good picture of whoever or whatever it is that we are researching.

In this step we'll dig into the primary areas of research. These areas are critical to gaining confidence and will ensure you won't waste time going down the wrong path. The areas include: researching your competition, your allies, your prospects, and yourself.

RESEARCH YOUR COMPETITION

In February of 2016, HBO interviewed NBA star Kobe Bryant about his retirement and his twenty-year career in the NBA. During the interview it caught my attention how Kobe was so aware of his competition at every age of his career.

He shared how at the age of eight he was already scoring sixty-three points in a single game. He figured out that kids weren't very good at dribbling the ball with their left hand so he'd let them dribble a few times with their right hand, and then using his body, he'd force them to switch hands. As soon as they did, they'd fumble the ball and Kobe would be there to knock it out and take over possession to score.

While in the NBA, he continued the process of researching his competition by studying footage of the previous season's championship team. There isn't anything unique to Kobe's process, but his desire to win drove him to research his competition, which resulted in five NBA championships.

Kobe was one of the best in the business because he was passionate about his work. Regardless of your industry, there will always be competition. Note that your competition may be found outside or inside your organization.

As you do your research on your competition, you will start to identify clear differences and similarities. You will begin to see your unique qualities, which will allow you to define what you bring to the world that makes you worth supporting. It is essential to know what is already out there. The more information you gather, the more confident you'll become around your product(s) and/or service(s). You should feel a sense of confidence knowing that you bring something special to your clients and community.

Your fundraising success depends heavily on you and your team making the right decisions based on the results of your research. If you set the date of your event on the same day as a well-established event or holiday in your community, your event is sunk before you've even begun. If your target audience tends to travel on the weekends, host your event during the week and not on the weekend while they are away.

If your audience enjoys spending time at home and they have young children, you'll want to accommodate your fundraiser to meet their lifestyle. Don't assume you have the right date and time, ask them. You can have the most incredible cause and event, but if your potential guests already have plans, they won't be at your event. If you do your research, you won't be nearing the event date wondering why no one has sent in their RSVP.

Just like my mentor asked me, I'm going to ask you to create your competition list. This list will include everyone you would consider competition. Remember, this doesn't necessarily have to be another nonprofit organization. This may be local entertainment such as a concert or sporting event, eating out, or donations to the church or school program. It may even be another event or individual within your own organization.

This was the process I used to research dinner events in my community. I started with a blank excel spreadsheet. In the first column I typed in every organization in town that hosted a dinner. I went online and printed off the event listings from local community event websites. I collected the socialite magazines and started pulling up the details I could find about other charity events in town.

What was their date?

Location?

Event chairman?

Table and ticket prices?

Total amount raised?

Who were their sponsors?

Who was the presenting sponsor?

Did they have a special project or restricted gift they were raising funds for?

Was their location unique?

Did they have a theme?

I put together as much information as I could find. Many of the columns were left blank due to lack of information from one source, but as I moved on to the next resource I found new details they shared. The purpose of this spreadsheet was to gather as much information as possible. I wanted to create clarity so I knew how to best create my own unique plan. Note that no decisions had been made at this stage. We did not have a date, location, event chairman, etc.

Let's change out the scenario and say you are an individual raising personal support. This spreadsheet is now a list of all the other individuals who may be serving in a similar geographic location. This may include individuals or organizations who receive support from your targeted prospect list.

How much are they trying to raise?

What information do you know about how they raised their support?

Are they fully funded?

How much time did it take them?

What do you know about who they are targeting for support?

Have they had success with corporate support? Support from organizations? Support from individuals/families?

RESEARCH YOUR ALLIES

If you are raising funds, you know hundreds of thousands of fundraisers have gone on before you. Some have done it well and others have not. Note that the basics of fundraising are the same regardless of whether it is for a social cause, healthcare organization, ministry, etc. The framework of the process is still the same.

As I made plans to put on a dinner event in my community, I knew that there were plenty of similar events in town and in other communities across the country. There are people in your industry who are doing great things and others who are just barely making it. Start surrounding yourself with those who are succeeding and figure out their playbook. Remember, you are the average of the five people you spend the most time with; go find and surround yourself with the best in your industry.

Pick up the phone, shoot out an email, study them, and find out why they are seeing growth. If you have the ability to schedule a call with them, make that appointment today. Start with flattery and ask for 30 minutes of their time to talk through how they got started.

Just be realistic about this person's time. If they are extremely busy you may have to schedule a meeting months in advance or have a phone conversation whenever it is convenient for them. That meeting may be very early in the morning, during your lunch hour, or in the evening. Do not turn down the opportunity to meet with them.

I found my ally at my nonprofit's national conference. It is not unusual to find the best in your industry at a conference, training, or webinar. The best leaders tend to rise to the surface because of their results. They can be easily identified within your organization because they frequently get asked to speak or lead trainings to share their success. This is an open door to have a conversation. After my frantic note taking in a breakout session, my gut told me I needed to do whatever I could to spend time with the lady who led the session.

I would recommend immediately introducing yourself if you are face to face, but in my case, I traveled home and sent her an email. In the email I wrote how much I enjoyed her session and how I was just creating my first event. We then scheduled a time to talk over the phone, and I asked her for specific information on how she created her structure that led to the success of her event.

She shared with me documents and resources that I never would have received in a training session, but because I asked for help, she was more than willing to email me the documents they used to get started. There is no need to recreate a document when you have someone in your industry who wants to see you succeed and has already done it. You can save yourself time and heartache if you just research your allies and ask for their help.

RESEARCH YOUR PROSPECTS

Your future prospects may be a corporation, a foundation, a donor, or a volunteer. If you don't take the time to learn more about the people around you, they will have a tendency to not want to take you seriously.

There are really only three kinds of prospects: a prospect who gives you (1) time; (2) money; or (3) in-kind resources. As you pull your research together, you are looking for any information that will tell you why this person would have the interest and the ability to do anything for you and your cause. If your prospect is missing either of these components, you may determine that they are no longer a good fit for your organization.

With the use of the Internet and social media, you can easily see what interests someone. Are they interested in family issues? Their kid's school? Their church or ministry work? The animal shelter? You are watching posts about the loss of a loved one, a child going off to college, pictures of pets, babies, the elderly, a family member who has been going through tough times or battling a disease...and the list goes on.

You start to gather that Sherlock Holmes research. How much free time do they have in this season of their life? It is your job to create broad observations from minute details until you have the ability to meet face-to-face to get more clarity.

It usually doesn't take much time to identify whether an individual may be interested or able to support your cause, because you've done your research. I'm not saying you should stalk your volunteers and donors, but I am saying that you need to care. If you don't care about their interests when you first meet them, you'll never understand fully what they are capable of doing for you and your organization.

Companies tend to be a little easier to research because many organizations are proud of their charity work and want the community to see the work they do, so they often post it online. Foundations are very similar. You tend to know from their website overview if they have an interest in your field of work. Don't waste your time or theirs if you are not a good fit. All it takes is a little research, and if you still aren't sure, a phone call will answer your remaining questions.

When you find the donors and volunteers who are a good fit, you'll know almost immediately. Don't get discouraged if you don't immediately get a warm fuzzy that they care about your cause. Sometimes you have to make them interested, and that may happen over time as they get to know you and the work you do. People give for many different reasons, and if you can identify their reason, you can give them reason to be interested. We'll go further into that in chapter 6.

As you dig into your research, one of the primary things to take note of is how your audience likes to receive communication. If you put a lot of energy into creating a print piece, you'll want to know that your audience actually reads it. You may only know the answer to that by asking.

Your research will help you to identify the best form of communication for your donor base, but more importantly, you need to be a great listener. They will give you hints to what they like and don't like, and that will open the door for more and better communication.

In my opinion, communication is best in the order listed below, with face-to-face communication being at the top of the list and a bulk newsletter at the bottom. Ask yourself how you would communicate with someone who is a friend. Would you mail them a formal piece of mail? Only you will know the answer to how to best communicate with each individual, organization, or corporation. The more time you invest to communicate, the more likely they will feel a part of your team and will want to contribute to your cause. If you ask someone to coffee or lunch, they will naturally be more invested because they gave you their time than someone who received a bulk letter in the mail and threw it in the trash.

Face-to Face

Phone Call

Video Chat

Text

Facebook Message

Social Media

Personal Email

Bulk Email

Handwritten Personal Letter/Card

Personal Letter

Bulk Letter

Bulk Newsletter

Know your competition and do your best not to reinvent the wheel. There is no reason to go down the same path and learn the hard way. Find out what works and pay attention to detail on how they communicate and interact with their supporters. Do not hesitate to call on your competition. You'd be surprised at how you may be able to collaborate and support each other.

RESEARCH YOURSELF

It seems a little strange to think about doing research on yourself, but you'd be surprised that after all the work you invest into this process, the primary reason for failure may be the person in your mirror. After resigning from my first two fundraising positions, I started to wonder if I was sabotaging my own success.

After burnout set in, I saw the pattern and realized I was the common element in both scenarios. No one made me work long hours or made me sacrifice time away from my family. I made those decisions. In this section of your research, I ask you to determine what kind of lifestyle you want to create as a nonprofit leader.

Let's chat about how to keep yourself in the game so you are there to achieve your vision. How many stories begin with a young man or woman who was on track to be the number one athlete or was moving up in their company or industry, but then something like injury or moral failure took them out of the game?

Greg Nuchols, the three-time world record holder in powerlifting, shared the secrets to winning his world records. He narrowed it down to success in three areas: (1) train consistently; (2) identify weaknesses; and (3) avoid injury.[3] Let's look at the three areas as they relate to fundraising.

1. **Train consistently.** Fundraising strategies are always changing. Our donor and volunteer prospects are continuously adapting to tactics used by our industry. Our job is to constantly be in training and be willing to change with the times. We have to be willing to be a student of our craft. Just when you think you've got it figured out, a new tool or resource will change the industry.

Don't allow you or your organization to become irrelevant because you got complacent.

Most entrepreneurs will acknowledge how important personal growth is to their success. This is true for the development industry as well. Only you can decide whether you want to invest your time and finances into training and improving your fundraising skills.

2. **Identify weaknesses.** One of the things I've learned over the years is that some people are naturally better at sharing their story than others. Some people have the ability to connect with most anyone they meet. Having a natural ability to connect with people does matter. If you have a dynamic personality you will have an easier time connecting with others, and therefore, raising more money.

   Some people just don't feel like they have the skill to raise money. My hope is that this book will help you identify your personal or organizational weaknesses so you can learn the skills to overcome them.

   Note: You may need to evaluate your specific approach and determine what feels the most natural to you. You do not want to feel like you are a multi-level marketer or a telemarketer. Your cause is too valuable and should be marketed as such. You are inviting others into the family.

3. **Avoid injury (burnout).** Those slated for championship titles of any sport or craft will reference injury as the result of what took them out of the game. If you become injured or got burnt out, you may become sidelined for months, years, or indefinitely.

A fundraiser will stay in his or her job for an average of 16 months[4], which tells me we have a serious injury problem in our industry. This number hit home for me when I realized I fell into those statistics. We have to protect ourselves from the injury of burnout because no one else will.

Just like a world champion athlete, your health is vital to your longevity, which results in your career success and long-term impact.

No one is forcing you to create and implement unsuccessful fundraising events. Half the battle is knowing what other successful fundraisers are doing. It is no surprise to me that when someone breaks a world record it shows a new generation of athletes how to take the sport to the next level.

Because it's been done, they know it's possible. This is no different for each of us as we dig into our craft and learn how to be the best in our industry. This is why research is so critical to the 7-Step process.

OVERCOME DESPERATION

Just like the dating game, desperation is not attractive. If you feel overwhelmed or are in a hopeless situation, it will take over your thoughts and actions. You behave differently when you feel the pressure to succeed, and if you are raising funds for your personal budget, it may mean the pressure to keep your job.

Desperation puts you in a position where you make poor decisions. If you have a limited amount of time and feel others breathing down your neck to make things happen, you'll get desperate, which results in unhealthy behaviors.

You may start to feel defensive and protective of every dollar spent, feeling as though your staff team is "stealing" or "hijacking" your donors. If a sponsor decides to support another event or department in your organization, you may start to harbor negative feelings towards a co-worker or feel like a victim.

Remember, your donors don't have to give to you nor do they have to give to your specific project within your organization. Donors should never feel pressured to know or understand your organization's staff assignments to raise funds.

As an organization grows in size, so do the budgets and staff assignments. Do your best to give off a united front that all donations are encouraged regardless of whether it helps your specific goal. Depending on the size of your organization, you may be responsible for the entire budget or you may have a portion of the funding responsibility. Donors should have the choice to give to any project of their choice without guilt from one of your staff.

Avoid desperation by not putting the pressure on. Think of all the worst-case scenarios that could happen. What if all things went wrong, what would happen to you? Your team? Your mission?

Earlier, I referred to an event that raised $500k in its first year and had three incredible back-to-back years. In year one, it brought in over $500k net. Year two, it jumped to $600k, and year three, it brought in $700k. But by year four, the writing was on the wall that $800k was not going to happen.

Our team was really hard on ourselves. It felt like we had failed. We had set the expectation that the event must get bigger and better every year, but that wasn't realistic. Our community was assessed to raise $50k in the first year and we raised $500k. Did I forget to mention we planned this event in 2007 and 2008, and then launched it in 2009, which were tough years for our country? We as a community were just starting to feel the effects from the downturn.

I recall having the conversation with my volunteers about why we were so disappointed in our results. We raised $600k, which was a lot of money! Other charities in town would have given anything for an event that net $600k. I understand that we all want to see growth year after year, but it's not practical to think that all years are going to see an upward swing. If you look at your country's economic grid, there are always going to be up and down swings in growth. I also believe that there are seasons where everything just clicks and your team is solid.

Desperation repels people, and they'll see it in your body language, how you act, and what you say. You'll start talking about what you "need" to raise during inappropriate situations like online, at family gatherings, or with people you just met, with little regard to how it is perceived. You'll create me-focused conversations without even knowing you're doing it, which will compromise your ability to serve and connect with others.

Here are some tips to use if you are feeling as though desperation has crept into your life.

First, acknowledge it. It will help you to understand and be aware of your feelings.

Second, ask yourself why you feel pressured. Are your feelings validated? The pressure may not even be coming from the work itself. It may be coming from your family and not necessarily from the job. Confiding in someone about the challenges will allow you to relieve the pressure and come to terms with the circumstances you are in. Once again, this is why a mentor or coach is so important. You don't want to lean on your potential donors and volunteers for this kind of support.

Third, go back to Step 1 and focus your vision. Are you getting distracted from your vision? There will be a lot of shiny objects along the way, but don't let that distract you from the end goal.

Finally, when you go in to meet with a potential donor, go in with confidence.

CREATE CONFIDENCE

Amy Cuddy, an American social psychologist, author and lecturer, did a TED talk in 2012 about nonverbal communication and quickly saw viral video success when over 33 million people viewed her talk. Amy started by offering a no-tech life hack. She encouraged her audience to change their posture for two minutes, and then shared how that hack "could significantly change how their lives unfold."[5]

Amy recommended a technique to improve your confidence in high-pressure situations, called *power posing*. She had done research and concluded that nonverbal expressions of power (open, space-occupying postures) affect people's feelings, behaviors, and hormone levels. She and a few colleagues did an experiment that showed adopting body postures associated with dominance and power ("power posing") for as little as two minutes can increase testosterone, decrease cortisol, increase appetite for risk, and cause better performance in job interviews.[6]

The philosophy is, if you act powerful, you can be powerful. Imagine someone who just won a marathon or completed an ironman competition. When they cross over the finish line, they have an open posture, with their hands open or pumped towards the sky and with their chin raised. This is the power pose. You are strong, confident, and accomplished, and everyone around you will see that radiate from you.

Amy actually recommended that you go to the restroom, close the stall, and get into the power pose, making yourself as expansive as possible for two minutes before a big meeting or presentation. The question she raised reflected back to the statement I made at the beginning of this book. Is it possible to fake it until you make it? The answer is *yes*.

If you are feeling pressured and stressed, you actually have the power to turn that around. Utilize these tools and eliminate the desperation in how you feel, act, and talk.

You should have a continuous desire to see to it that your research is always up to date. Most fundraisers will put on the same event annually, and the challenge you have to avoid is getting stuck in a rut. It's not okay to put the event on autopilot after you host your first event. You may have invested the time and done the research before your first event, but you will also need to do the research for year two, three, and every year thereafter.

As you know, your research will never end because people and supporters will naturally come and go. We are also living in a changing world where new technology and resources are made available every day. This is not the time to sit back and put your fundraising on autopilot.

Now that you know your competition, your allies, your prospects, and yourself, let's go build out your team!

CHAPTER 3

STEP 3: ENLIST YOUR TEAM

I was in my mid-twenties and felt completely out of place, but I agreed to attend a networking luncheon to promote the ALS Association. I had my official nametag on and was wearing professional business attire. I felt like a kid, but I tried hard to just fly under the radar. Events like this were always a little awkward but effective, and I needed to put myself out there if I was going to get anyone involved in my organization.

I sat down next to a woman who I had met a handful of times. She was confident, and I watched from a distance as she made conversation with several people in the room. I listened in as she shared a story about a recent meeting with the CEO of the largest company in town.

A few minutes later, she started up a conversation with me, asking questions about my role in the organization and the work I did. During our conversation she made a comment about how she knew "everyone in this town." I smiled back at her, shaking my head to agree that I'm sure she did. That statement was forever ingrained in my memory.

Time passed and two years later, I was interviewing for a new fundraising position. I couldn't help but reflect back to that first interview and the water bottle that stood in my way. I thought to myself that nothing was going to stop me from this opportunity. I now had six years of experience and my confidence was much stronger.

I passed the first interview and moved on to the second interview. I thought the water bottle was tough, but this organization wanted me to come back and present them with the best duct tape fundraiser. Yes, a fundraiser using duct tape. I came in confident and prepared, and I was not about to let another sales presentation take me down. When the job offer came in, I couldn't help but feel a sense of redemption. All my hard work and determination had paid off.

The American Cancer Society was a billion-dollar non-profit[1], and within two weeks, I was on a plane to a conference to listen to the CEO share his vision for the organization. Sitting in that room, I knew I was a part of something world changing. I was a part of fulfilling the vision of a world without cancer.

I returned home from that conference feeling empowered as a member of the team. I knew the mission before I got there, but now I knew the vision. I also knew that a $25,000-event in my town was just not going to cut it. My vision needed to scale up to match their vision. I needed to surround myself with the strongest leaders in the organization who were putting on the largest events. I needed to spend time with the most well respected individuals within the organization and align myself with them.

I quickly learned that our organization had an event in Chicago, IL that had just raised $1.8 million in their first year. Tyler, TX, a community closer to the size of my town in Springfield, MO, had just raised $1 million. I was also aware that the largest single event was being held in Dallas, TX. It was in its 36th year and raised nearly $4 million that previous year.

I thought to myself, "If they can do it, why can't we? We're going to raise $1 million!" I truly believed we could raise a million dollars. Why couldn't we? At this stage I had zero volunteers, no team, no plan, but I was convinced I wasn't going to set this event up for anything less. My vision was clear—a world without cancer—and I was focused on it.

I went to work to implement Step 2 by running my research on these three events in Chicago, Tyler, and Dallas. Through my research I identified several factors that created their success, but one of the common threads was their team, and more importantly, their key volunteer leadership, their chairmen.

I spent days digging through the research. I needed to find an event chair and I knew I couldn't figure this out on my own. I reached out to a few leaders I knew who had helped me on previous events, but one voice kept ringing in my ears.

"I know everyone in this town!"

So I picked up the phone and called her. What would it hurt? At this point I didn't know if she cared about the fight against cancer, but honestly, I didn't care and I needed to exhaust every avenue if this was going to happen.

Weeks passed before she returned my call. She said, "I am so sorry, I have been so busy, but I got your message. What's going on?" I went on to tell her about the opportunity I was given to join the American Cancer Society and start a new event in our community.

During our short call I mentioned that we didn't have to start entirely from scratch. There were several events that had seen success within our organization, but our options were open. If we wanted to go black tie, create a whiteout party, a themed event of any kind, we had the ability to do that. She said she'd do a little digging and she'd get back with me.

The first call took two weeks for a returned call, but this one only took minutes. I was surprised when my phone rang and she was on the other end. This call was very different. Her tone was completely different. She was fired up. She had hung up the phone and jumped online to look up the Cattle Baron's Ball where she found our $4 million Dallas event.

She said, "Do you know how big this event is?"

Of course I knew, but that event was in its 36th year and I truly thought a western-themed event would never fly in our community. She thought I was crazy and went on to talk about how our community was big in agriculture and it would be ridiculous to not do this event.

I thought to myself, she's right. Why wouldn't we just recreate the event? We had all the resources and tools to make the event a success. We had access to volunteers, corporate leaders, and the staff leadership. So without hesitation, I asked for her help, and she became my one, my team captain, the event chair.

IT ONLY TAKES ONE

It only takes one volunteer to get started. I hear it often from fundraisers that fundraising is overwhelming. They say, "I don't know anyone who would want to give to my cause. I don't even know where to start." You start with one. It doesn't matter if you are starting a board of directors, an advisory group, or an event-planning committee. It only takes one.

Start by identifying the reasons why someone would say yes. The most common include:

- They want to give back.
- They want to use their skills and talents to benefit others.
- They want to see personal growth in their life.
- They want to build new friendships/meet new people (possibly in a new city).
- They want to learn new things.
- They want to be recognized and have a sense of achievement.
- They want to make a difference.
- They want to have a good time and volunteering is fun!
- They want to build their Rolodex.
- They want to do something meaningful.
- They want to gain new skills and build their resume.
- They were asked!

Let's say you go to the local YMCA to play a game of basketball. When you get to the court you notice another guy shooting hoops at the same net. You probably wouldn't think much to ask if he wants to play one-on-one.

You look down to the other end of the court and see a couple others shooting ball, so you holler down, "Hey, do you guys want to play a game?" Before you know it, you have two teams, and others start to watch from the sidelines wishing they could get into the game because you are all having so much fun.

Fundraising is just like a game of basketball or any other team sport. For the sake of the example, let's pretend you are the head coach of the team. Your "job" is to recruit the team. Someone either hired or recruited you because they saw that you were a strong leader and could build a team that could win.

Because you were tasked with the job, you start with Step 1 with the vision to have a winning team, Step 2 to run your research, and Step 3 to enlist the players for your team. As the coach, which position is the most important to fill? You should start with the position of the team captain.

When you begin your team captain search, you start by identifying the qualities you want in a strong team leader. The best team captains tend to be competitive, hardworking, encouraging, highly respected, and pas-sionate about the game.

I'd like to remind you that the enlisting or recruiting process goes both ways. Just as you are looking for a strong leader, that individual will be looking for a strong leader in you. If you and the team captain are not a good fit, no competitive, hardworking, encouraging individual will be successful. All members of the team are important, including you.

I mentioned that for this example you are playing the role of the coach, which means you won't have the ability to play in the game. That may make you freak out for a second, but imagine what your team would look like if you are not the team captain or the quarterback. You must recruit someone for this position.

Most fundraisers are used to playing the lead role, but Step 3 of the fundraising freedom plan is to enlist your team and not be the team. This is not a solo sport, and you are not the team captain. You are the coach.

You will have a say in how the plays are made, but your team captain and the team will execute the plan. You will be responsible for the most important part of the plan, which is to enlist, coach, and train the team. No one will know your organization as well as you do. Your role is vital to winning, but your volunteers will be playing the game and therefore executing the plan.

Remember that no one typically shows up to play in a league and asks to be the team captain. So if you think the best recruitment tool is to post an ad in the newspaper or recruit your team online using social media, think again. When you join a team for the first time it is typically a pretty uncomfortable experience. You most likely won't know the people in the group. You'll probably be more quiet than normal and will evaluate the coach and assess how the team is run.

Very rarely do you hear someone say, "I'm in charge. Everyone can follow me now." It just doesn't work that way. Most people want to be asked, and if they do volunteer themselves for the role, they may or may not be the right fit for the role. Your "one" is critical to your future success so it's important that you have the right person in the position.

Your team captain should be researched, evaluated, and recruited because they are the best person for the job. You only have one position to fill, and once it's filled you won't want to move them out if someone better comes along. The pressure is on to ensure this individual or couple is a good fit. You, your event, the board of directors, and ultimately your organization's future success will weigh heavily on this one decision.

FIND YOUR LEAD VOLUNTEER

We often tell ourselves the lie that no one will be interested in volunteering for our cause because it isn't as compelling as sick kids, puppies, or fill in the blank with your favorite charity. Remember, the person you are looking to enlist as your team captain (i.e. your event chairman, advisory group chair, or the chairman of the board) may or may not know you or that your charity exists today. That's okay.

Your research in Step 2 will give you the confidence to know whether you should pursue an individual team captain prospect. If someone aligns with your organization's values and vision, your job as the coach is to convince them that they should play for your team.

Throw out all your thoughts about who would or wouldn't be interested in your cause. If you have a winning team and you are a good coach, you will recruit and motivate the team captain and the members of your team to want to be on your team and support your cause.

Have you ever noticed that there are movie directors like Martin Scorsese, Stephen Spielberg, and Ron Howard who have the ability to recruit top talent to their movies year after year? They've been able to replicate success in many of their projects because they've gained a reputation for being the best and for recruiting the best.

As your team's coach, if you are not a good leader, you are not going to put together a winning team by chance. If you don't feel confident that you can lead a team to raise the funds you see in your vision, it's time to pick up some books on leadership. You may not have the skills today, but you can definitely become a stronger leader with practice and with the drive to get better.

Other comments from fundraisers may sound something like, "I can't believe they raised that much. Our cause is so much more important." It's hard to believe we will tear down each other's causes or create a ranking of worthy and unworthy charities.

The question is not whether the cause is important. The question is, "Is your cause worth someone else's time, energy, and financial resources?" You may have an amazing cause, but if you appear dysfunctional, distracted, and unorganized, no one will follow you and say yes to your team.

Many people look at large-scale fundraisers and think they were an overnight success. Think again. A celebrity rarely joins on as a charity spokesperson without some convincing. Somewhere along the line you'll find a fundraiser, a nonprofit leader, or a high level volunteer who had a vision, did their research, and enlisted the celebrity to their team!

Some charities can move at a faster pace because they have a compelling cause, but I guarantee you that behind all good fundraisers there was an extraordinary team led by an extraordinary team captain and an extraordinary coach.

The characteristics you should be looking for in your team captain may include the following. They...

- Are passionate
- Are driven
- Desire to build strong relationships
- Care about others
- Are a team player
- Are well liked
- Are upbeat and positive
- Won't quit or shy away from difficult situations

- Are a natural leader but willing to take direction
- Have a pattern of success with whatever they are a part of
- Are not afraid to ask others for financial support or resources
- Have values that align with your organization
- Have the time to invest and may have had a recent life change (kids went off to college, entered retirement, resigned from a job, etc.)
- Have the ability to make a personal and/or corporate financial contribution
- Are well connected
- Are well respected
- Have professional skills to do the job

Make a list of ten to twenty people who could take you or your organization on to the next level. Remember, these are people who may or may not care about your organization today. We'll discuss how to engage them later.

To help you think through where to find these individuals, let's talk through some options. This individual may be in upper level management serving in the top or second tier of the company. It's common to want to recruit the CEO or top executive of a company, but the number two executive may have more time available to dedicate to your cause and may be in line to be the next CEO or executive director of the company or organization. They also may have access to influence the CEO and secure funds from the company.

Your one may be the spouse of an influential community or organizational leader. This individual typically has the same access to their high profile spouse's contacts and has been on the journey with their spouse to motivate and drive them to their current position. If their spouse thinks big, they most likely have the same ability to think big.

Your one will typically show leadership skills in other areas of their lives like the PTA, their family, community events, etc. Think back to the conversations you've had with individuals. Your number one may already be in your life. They may be someone who shows the most interest in the work you do. They could be your top cheerleader and already support your cause. This individual could already be a standout within your organization, but you've never asked them to serve in a leadership capacity.

You may also find your one serving in a small or large role with other organizations, their church, school, or community. If this is a large-scale leadership position, look for individuals who have chaired or served on other boards. This is not a requirement, but if they've served on other boards it will tell you that they enjoy working in leadership and have the skill to serve at this level within your organization.

A+ VOLUNTEERS

Identifying the right team member is one of the most important factors in your future success. Feel free to use whatever scale you feel most comfortable with, but for the sake of our example I'm going to use the academic grading system of A, B, C, D, and F to identify the team members' level of skill.

Letter Grade	Percentage	GPA
A	90-100	4.0
B	80-89	3.0
C	70-79	2.0
D	60-69	1.0
F	0-59	0.0

As you get more skilled at this, you can move to a more detailed system with + and − added.

Letter Grade	Percentage	GPA
A+	95%-100%	4.33/4.00
A	93%-94%	4.00/4.00
A-	90%-92%	3.67/4.00
B+	87%-89%	3.33/4.00
B	83%-86%	3.00/4.00
B-	80%-82%	2.67/4.00
C+	77%-79%	2.33/4.00

C	73%-76%	2.00/4.00
C-	70%-72%	1.67/4.00
D+	67%-69%	1.33/4.00
D	63%-66%	1.00/4.00
D-	60%-62%	0.67/4.00
F	0%-59%	0.00/4.00

You can see that each grade has a percentile attached to give you a gauge as to where this team member fits in regards to the overall pool of individuals in your community or target geographic area.

As you can imagine, you want as many A's on your team as possible. If I'm putting together a team, I want my team made up of A and B level team members and less from the D and F pool. Each organization is going to have different criteria for what makes up an A or B level individual. You may have a make-or-break item on your list of criteria that immediately makes a candidate a C level team member.

Depending on the type of team member you are looking for, you can start to place your ideal candidates at the top of the grading scale. If I'm looking to fill the chair or one position, I'm going to be looking for a high profile individual in the community who has the time and energy to invest in our cause, but is also well respected and whose morals and values align with the work we are doing. Even if an A+ team member may have had 75% of the criteria but had a recent run-in with the law, their grade could instantaneously drop to a C or D level member because of that incident.

The premise here is to identify the qualities that make up your ideal team members, and then commit to only enlist members that meet your A or B level. The reason for scaling your volunteers using this system will also come into play as they enlist others to the team.

Let's say you are an A+ level member of the team as the CEO of a large corporation. As the CEO, you have influence over the top tier leadership of your company all the way down to the hourly employees. You also have influence over other CEO's in your community. This means that you have a high likelihood or have the ability to recruit other A+ level volunteers/donors as well as recruit A, A-, B+, B, B-, etc.

Now let's say you are a C level team member. You found an ad in the paper asking for volunteers or you were looking for a service project, so you called and asked to help out. You may be highly motivated to help and serve, but you do not have many connections in the community and you don't have the ability to give. Who do you think you'll recruit to the team? As a C level, you'll recruit maybe a B or B-, but more likely you'll find yourself recruiting your peers at the C or C- level. This is the group you will likely have the most influence over.

As you can see, the more A+ level team members you recruit, the more influence and alignment your team will have to the vision, and those A+ level team members will in turn recruit high level supporters to your team.

It's easy to slip past this recruitment tool, but the more time you work on assessing your team members using this scale, the greater the likelihood you'll have the right individuals sitting around the table when you go ask for financial support. Each member of the team must bring valuable assets to the group that allow for growth and increased support from others on your target prospect list.

Be sure you have a place on your team for volunteers at all levels. There should be a place for everyone to get plugged in. Just remember not to invite a D level individual to serve on your leadership team with your A and B volunteers. The A and B level volunteers will question your leadership and will step down. This is great way to kill your fundraising campaign before it even begins.

Every position of your team is crucial to your success. The last thing you want to handle is unnecessary drama or the firing of a volunteer because they weren't assessed properly for the team. If you handpick your leadership, you will be thankful years down the road when you have a team that is high functioning and focused on the vision.

ASK YOUR LEAD VOLUNTEER

Now that you've identified who could be your one or lead volunteer, it's time to enlist them.

Did you know there are approximately 1,000 sports scouts in the United States alone?[2] Almost every industry hires staff whose purpose is to evaluate talent before they move on to the next level. This is the process I recommend you establish for your organization as well. The more elite the pool is, the more honored you are to be a part of it.

First of all, this is one of the most critical positions on your team, so do not take this process lightly. This person's name should have come up several times in conversation. When you ask others who they think would be a good fit for the position, the same few names should have come to the surface.

Narrow down your list to your top three names and determine how and who can gain access to this person.

> Is it someone you personally know?
>
> Is it a friend of a friend?
>
> Is it a celebrity figure?

Determine who would be the best person to make the call or make the first contact. This is important. You may only have one shot at it. Once the individual finds out you are trying to recruit them, they'll either feel honored or targeted. They may choose not to respond to your calls. If this is the case, don't feel rejected. It may not be the right timing and you may need to try again.

Okay, you've identified the best person to make contact with the first person on your list. Now it's time to make the call, send the email, or shoot over the text. You or the person you enlisted to make contact with this individual should know how to best reach out and communicate with this person. If this were a friend, you wouldn't send a formal email or letter to request a meeting; instead, you'd pick up the phone or send them a text to find a time to meet.

If you are recruiting someone to serve on the board or to lead an important committee, this request should be done face-to-face if possible. I understand you may be recruiting someone from a different part of the state or country and seeing them in person is just not possible. In that case, a phone call or video call would be the next best option.

You may be thinking to yourself, "Why would anyone say yes?" They are going to say yes because it is an honor. They are flattered that you thought of them and that their peers nominated them for the position.

If you beg them to serve in this role, they will feel the heaviness of the time commitment and the burden the project may be on their life. You will also regret recruiting a leader who had to be coerced and who lacked the passion and dedication you need for the position.

Here are two options to consider:

Option 1: They were nominated, and you are excited to offer them the opportunity to serve in this position. No one could do the project better than them. It is an honor to invite them to lead the team.

Option 2: You knew they would say yes if you asked. You didn't want to take the time or take on the fear of rejection if you asked anyone else. No one else would do it.

What feelings come to mind when you read Option 1 versus Option 2?

Which scenario would you want to walk into?

If your team captain, your "one," doesn't feel special, why would anyone else on your team feel special or, for that matter, want to join your team?

Prior to going into this meeting, you want to go back to Step 1 to review your vision. Does this person align with your vision? When you were brainstorming with those you trust about who could take on this role, you all must have agreed that this individual or couple aligned with your vision and had the capacity to fulfill the position.

You then went on to Step 2 to do your research about them. You tried to find the skeletons in their closet. Do their values align with yours? Do they have the capacity to fulfill the job? The more you think about it, the more you realize that this person is special and that they wouldn't have made your top 3 list if you didn't think they were a good fit.

Wouldn't you feel honored if someone took that much time to match up your gifts and talents, and felt like you were a good fit for the position?

Imagine someone approached you with this frame of mind. It would be hard for you to say no, correct? That's exactly the environment you want to create. The larger the responsibility, the increased amount of time you should invest in researching this individual and ensuring they are a good fit for the position. You do not want a warm butt in this seat.

Think of some of the most critical roles in government, corporations, organizations, etc. Those individuals were groomed, trained, and elected to their positions. They spent years of training to even be considered. The application process was elaborate and the candidate pool was elite. Why should your organization expect anything less?

WE ARE BETTER TOGETHER

Competitions are held around the world to determine which horse is the strongest. Out of all the breeds, the Belgian draft horse was named the largest and strongest. One single Belgian horse could pull 8,000 pounds on its own. If two Belgians are harnessed together you would think they'd pull a total 16,000 pounds, which would be twice their weight seeing that you have two horses. The results showed that the Belgian draft horse pulled not two times as much, but three times as much, pulling 20,000 to 24,000 pounds.

Even more impressive about these same two Belgian horses is that if they have trained together and are unified working toward one single goal of pulling weight, they begin to think as one and can pull almost four times as much as a single horse, pulling 30,000 to 32,000 pounds.[3]

I know we are not Belgian draft horses, but imagine how much you could accomplish if you had one person you could lock arms with and move in one direction as one solid unit. You could produce nearly four times the results. Let's look at that from a very basic scale. You, as an individual, have the ability of raising $1, but by linking arms and minds with just one other, your team captain (your "one"), you could raise $4 with the same amount of energy.

If you only take one piece of advice from this book, this is it. You need just one! Do not go this alone. If you care about your mission and you want results, this is how you do it.

Who is your "one" that can walk side by side with you on this journey?

I recently watched CBS correspondent Charlie Rose as he interviewed Apple's design chief, Jony Ive. During the interview, they discussed the secrecy of the work done by Apple and about Jony's team. Jony shared that over the course of fifteen years, only two of his twenty-two designers left the company. After working together for that long, I imagine Jony's team had the synergy of a group of Belgian draft horses. You only have to look at Apple's product sales to see how well this team has done.

Jony shared how hard they worked to create innovative new products, some of which would never be seen. They followed the vision of Apple to ensure only the best products like the iPod, iPhone, and iPad were released to the world, and they enlisted only the best team members to be a part of the team.[4]

This is why every member of your team is essential to your success. You want the sharpest, most driven, hard-working individuals who believe they are about to create something that will forever change the world. What if you had the most influential people in your community sitting around a table discussing how they could best support your cause? How they could create more impact and influence through your work?

We all want to be a part of a winning team, and so do your volunteers. Why is your event or cause not worthy of the best? Why should other charities be featured on national television? Why not you? Why not your next event?

What if you and your team consistently came together with a drive and passion knowing that you "get to" impact lives?

Could you imagine the impact and change that would happen if everyone was equipped and trained for the job they were in?

A good team is only good if everyone on the team is moving in the same direction and if every member is willing to make decisions based on the greater good of the entire team. If you lack a good vision and never did your research before you recruited your team, you won't be pulling in the same direction and your $1 will never turn into $4. The mission and vision statements you created should give you the clarity you need so that everyone is 100% on board before they are ever invited to sit at the table.

That clarity will also ensure you trust your team members, which will eliminate micromanaging your team. Because of that, everyone will be free to run at their own pace and far surpass your expectations of them. If your vision is to eradicate a disease or eliminate poverty, it really doesn't matter how you get there as long as you get there, right? Your team won't let you down if you are all working towards the same mission and vision.

Imagine you are running in a marathon and the path isn't clearly marked out. You trained, you prepped, and you paid the fees. What if the organizers were so concerned about taking your money that they forgot to mark the roads to show you the finish line? How frustrated would you be? You'd probably figure it out, and most likely you'd make your way to the finish line, but not without being extremely upset with the leadership.

You are the leader. You are responsible for the vision... the finish line. Put your race map together and do the research to be sure all the roads are clearly marked so no one gets frustrated or confused.

CHAPTER 4
STEP 4: ENHANCE YOUR BRAND

"At the end of the day people won't remember what you said or did, they will remember how you made them feel." – Maya Angelou

When I was thirteen, my family loaded up in our '85 Chevy Caprice station wagon and went on a road trip to Seattle, Washington to visit my sister. On our vacation we went into a popular local coffee shop at Pike Place Market called Starbucks.

When you hear the name Starbucks I'm sure you have a picture and feeling that immediately come to mind. Can you smell the coffee? Can you see the logo? What kind of feeling comes over you? That "feeling" is not an accident. The Starbucks' leadership created that specific feeling for their customers when they built out the Starbucks brand.

This "feeling" is what I want you to create as you enhance your brand here in Step 4. Starbucks isn't known for having the best coffee, but that hasn't stopped anyone from buying it because of the way it makes them feel. If I'm at the airport or if it's cold and I'm near a Starbucks, I can almost envision my day going better because that cup is in my hand. I know what I'm going to get with a cup of Starbucks coffee, and they've fulfilled the expectation I have when I purchase a cup of coffee.

Howard Schultz, Starbucks President and CEO, defined their company atmosphere when he said, "We're in the business of human connection and humanity, creating communities in a third place between work and home." Schultz and his leadership team at Starbucks came together as a team to identify exactly what they wanted to create for their customers, "a community in a third place." I want you to figure out how you can bring life to your brand.[1]

When someone thinks of you, what sort of feelings do you think come to their mind? Are these the feelings you want them to have? If not, now is the time to enhance your brand and create exactly what you want them to feel.

You have the same ability Starbucks has regardless of how new or old your organization is today. You may be a part of a larger organization that controls the national branding, but you have control over how you are perceived within your community, region, or state.

Can you think of a company or restaurant where at one location they are truly exceptional in customer service, cleanliness, and presentation, and that same business has a second location across town where you'd never step foot again because of how poorly it is run? This is what I'm talking about. You have a lot of control over your personal brand and the brand of the organization you represent.

This chapter and step play an important role in creating your future success. If you don't know who you are and don't have the ability to tell your story well, how will anyone else know how great you are?

Now that you've come through the vision, research, and team enlisting steps, you should have a good picture of who you are and what makes you stand out from your competition. All the information you've gathered will be extremely valuable as you nail down your branding.

Work with your lead volunteer to craft your message that shares how your work is unique and special, and then express that through your branding and image. In this step, we'll dig into your personal brand, your organizational brand, your logo, print materials, and website.

The goal is to differentiate your brand with the brand of your competitors. Over time, you and your organization's image should give your team and all those who come in contact with it a feeling of credibility, quality, and satisfaction. At a glance, the community and your target audience should be able to identify who you are with little explanation. Of course, all that will take time, but remember, your long-term goal is to make your brand a household name for your target audience.

There's a lot we can learn from companies like Starbucks. In the five years prior to our visit to Seattle in the late 80s and early 90s, Starbucks went from making $1.3 million a year to over $73 million.[2] At the end of 2015, the company reported revenue at $19.2 billion[3] with a "b."

The vision of Starbucks is "to establish Starbucks as the premier purveyor of the finest coffee in the world while maintaining our uncompromising principles while we grow." It is not by chance that their vision remains true today as they've grown from 17 stores in 1987 to 23,921[3] stores in 2016.[2]

As you can see, Starbucks didn't explode to what it is today by accident. Let's look at Starbucks through the lens of the 7 Steps to Fundraising Freedom. They had focus on their vision (Step 1). They ran their research (Step 2).

They enlisted a topnotch team (Step 3). They enhanced and built a strong brand (Step 4). They deployed their team members (Step 5). They asked you to buy their coffee (Step 6), and they made a difference in the lives of their customers by replicating the experience over and over again (Step 7). We'll dive deeper into the other steps in the upcoming chapters, but I wanted to give you a glimpse into where we are heading.

Images are powerful, and they can make or break your future growth. When you shop at your favorite store, you have expectations of what that experience will look and feel like, and ultimately, it plays a part in why you have become a repeat customer.

CREATE A PERSONAL BRAND

First impressions only happen once. You get just 7 seconds to make a good first impression.[4] You will be sized up primarily by your appearance, your handshake, and anything you say within those first 7 seconds.

It doesn't matter how strong a brand you are representing if you don't have a strong personal brand. I understand this is a book about fundraising, but anyone in sales will tell you that if you don't dress the part, the sale is at risk.

I know it's hard to think of yourself as a salesperson, but you are definitely in the business of sales. You may be selling hope, quality of life, a cure, or changed lives. You have a huge responsibility to positively represent your brand to the best of your ability.

Here are a few tips to remember as you build your personal brand. Dress to match your audience. How you present yourself matters. Do your homework and dress like your potential donor or volunteer. If you are meeting with the CEO of a corporation and they are always in a business suit, do not show up in jeans and a t-shirt. The opposite is also true. You don't want to show up overdressed for the occasion. If in doubt, always come dressed more professional than less professional.

Be prepared. Know your audience and plan ahead for what your day looks like. You never want to turn down a meeting because you aren't appropriately dressed or you're unprepared to present your cause. As a fundraiser, it is important to dress every day as if a donor meeting is just a phone call away.

Be aware of odors. When you meet with a volunteer or donor, be aware of strong smells like perfume, cologne, bad breath, cigar or cigarette smoke. Everyone has a different sensitivity to smell.

Details matter. You'd be surprised how quickly we evaluate each other. Pay attention to details such as wrinkled clothes, scuffed shoes, overdoing the jewelry or makeup. For men, this also includes being clean-shaven, combing or cutting your hair. Being laid back may be okay depending on your line of work, but it may not be appropriate to a volunteer or donor you want to recruit.

Definitions of attire may differ by the community. Note that business casual may mean one thing in your community, but if you travel across the country it may mean something entirely different. Bring a change of clothes, or pack a blazer or suit jacket if you are unsure.

Close your eyes and picture the leader of an organization or group you admire and aspire to be like. Now picture yourself as the leader of your organization. Do you present yourself the same way as that individual you admire? If you want to see similar success, how will your personal brand need to change? Imagine what the personal brand of a leader would need to look like if they were raising $1,000, $10,000, $100,000 or $1 million. Start making steps towards building a personal brand that represents the leader you want to become.

CREATE AN ORGANIZATIONAL BRAND

Now that you have a strong personal brand, you can move on to creating a strong organizational brand. When you begin this process, it is important that you've already enlisted your lead volunteer. Your lead volunteer and your team are an essential part to the branding process.

Here are a few reasons why:

- Asking the team for their opinion creates buy-in.
- They get to be a part of the fun stuff.
- By asking for their feedback, you show that you care about their opinion and want their input.
- You don't make important decisions without their knowledge. This doesn't mean you need them to sign off before moving forward; this means that you cared enough to tell them that a decision was about to be made.
- You are part of a team, and if each member of the team is expected to sell the brand and use the materials you've created, they will feel much more empowered if they had a say in it.
- They will help shape your image because they will bring an outside perspective you can't offer to your organization. You may think your logo is amazing, but if they see something else, others will too!

The design phase is one of my very favorite parts of the process. You are at the point where your ideas start to take shape and become tangible in graphics, pictures, and colors. It's like meeting a baby for the first time after nine months of preparing for their arrival. You had an idea of what they might look like, but this is the first time you get to physically see them. It should be a special moment.

When I started my own business and had my logo designed and put on business cards, print materials, and on a website, reality kicked in that this was actually happening. It was no longer just a vision; it was truly coming alive before my eyes.

I recall telling my husband, who is also my graphic designer, while he was creating my materials, "You are making me look too professional!" That's right, I told him he was making me look too professional. I'm shaking my head now at the thought of that comment coming out of my mouth.

He was able to capture the feeling I wanted as a fund-raising professional. My husband knew my brand. For most organizations, they don't have the problem of looking too professional; they have the problem of not looking professional enough. Unprofessional print pieces, low-resolution graphics, and poorly designed logos tell your audience a lot about who you are.

You are probably working on a tight budget and not hiring the best designer, but rather, the designer you can afford. I encourage you to take the time and invest in quality, professional design work. Remember, this is your first impression to everyone who encounters you or your organization, including all your donor prospects. Hiring a professional designer will be worth the investment.

You have plenty of options so don't feel like you have to hire the most expensive design firm in town. There are online companies who will design your logo or piece inexpensively, and you won't have to pay for it if you don't like it. Be sure to shop around and get quotes on your larger projects. The primary challenge you have is to organize your thoughts so the designer can get your ideas on paper without you changing your mind multiple times, costing you both time and money.

When you arrive at the branding step, your vision, research, and team will give you the support to create strong images that align with your cause. When you enlisted your team, you may have been able to recruit a designer to be a part of your volunteer committee. This would be a great addition to your team to have a professional design volunteer willing to donate their time. This will drastically cut your costs and create consistency for future pieces if they align with your organization long term.

I'm a huge fan of recruiting a design company to give an in-kind donation of time, but just remember, there is a difference between a volunteer who dabbles in design work and someone who has a design degree and does this as a career. When something is free, you may get what you pay for. Once again, don't be afraid to spend a little money on this. It will be worth the extra expense in the long run to ensure you have long-lasting designs that can grow with you and your organization.

Remember that designers, whether they are graphic designers, web designers or illustrators, are artists. It is important to be as up front as possible with your expectations so that you get the best results. Not every designer will be a good match with your work style. Don't be afraid to part ways if you don't mesh with your designer. Finding the right fit will reduce your stress and anxiety, and will ultimately result in a better outcome.

CREATE A HIGH QUALITY LOGO

You or your organization may or may not have a current logo today. You may have an organizational logo but are lacking a strong logo for your event, division, or individual brand. You'll notice that logos are used not only as a strong branding tool for your organization, but also as a strong branding tool for your programs and services.

Companies will typically utilize an iconic logo. For example, Nike typically uses the swoosh graphic or their name in type. They also have their Jordan line of products that uses their Michael Jordan logo with the graphic of Michael flying through the air to dunk a basketball. The same goes for nonprofits like the American Heart Association. They will use their signature heart logo, but will use unique branding for their Go Red for Women events and the Heart Walk.

A logo is more than a circle with your name written in the middle with a fancy font. The best way to start is with the brainstorming process. Ask yourself some important questions, including:

- How will the logo be used? (Advertising, billboards, letterhead, website, print materials, promotional items, t-shirts, mugs, stickers, invitations)
- What feeling do I want my audience to get when they see it? (Whimsical, strong, empowering, feminine, masculine, childlike)
- Decide if you want your name in the logo (American Cancer Society, Salvation Army) or a design with the text separate from the logo (Ronald McDonald House, Boys & Girls Clubs).

- What is your organization's color scheme and can you get that color on all your branded materials? (Heart Association – red, Breast Cancer Research Foundation – pink, Girl Scouts – green)

Tips for making a great logo[5]:

- Color
- Motion (Twitter)
- Two pictures wrapped in one (double entendre)
- Don't get caught in a design trend
- The art is something you can own (graphic stands out only because you made it stand out)
- Avoid a fancy font with your name
- Don't overthink it (Apple, Nike swoosh)
- People like symmetry (it's an OCD thing)
- Your logo should have a story

I encourage you to have multiple logos designed for you, your project or organization. When you have it narrowed down to three designs, share the decision-making process with your lead volunteer(s). Give them the opportunity to share their first impressions of each design. Chances are, they will give you the honest feedback you are looking for.

If there is a design you are leaning toward, it's okay to share that, but I encourage you to allow room for open communication to ensure the best results. When the decision is made, everyone in the room will know they've had a say in it and will therefore own the decision and support the design that was chosen.

CREATE A ONE-PAGE DOCUMENT

This is an essential presentation piece that should be in your toolbox. When you have the opportunity to meet one-on-one with a potential donor, you don't want to come in with a big presentation binder or a power point presentation. After all, if this were a "friend" you are building a relationship with, it would be awkward to pull out a lengthy sales presentation packet.

A one-pager should be more than enough space to share three basic pieces of information so anyone can get others involved.

1. Who are you?
2. The project or program's what, when, why, and where.
3. How can they help?

Know your audience and do your research to find out if this document is being presented to an individual or a group of individuals. You want to be sure your primary audience is receiving the information they want and need before you present the document.

I recently presented my materials to a Fortune 100 company. Prior to submitting my organization's information, I had the opportunity to speak with the chair of the company's community relations committee. During our conversation she was very clear on how she wanted me to submit our materials. She asked for a very concise one-page document that gave a history of our involvement with the company.

They wanted to know if their company had ever given to our organization in the past. If so, how were they involved? Had their employees supported our organization in the past? If so, how much did the employees contribute? How many years had they been involved? All this information was important to their committee to make a decision on whether they would give again.

When I received their email to confirm they would be funding my event, the chairman of the group told me that this was the best one-page document she had received from any charity to date. That compliment did not come as a surprise to me, but it was extremely flattering because I worked hard on the materials I sent over. Prior to submitting my request, I had run my research and I enlisted a volunteer from their company.

When they gave me their guidelines, I immediately contacted my volunteer from their company to review the materials before I submitted my request. Recruiting the right team and then inviting them to be a part of the process could be the difference between getting funded or not. After I received the confirmation email, I immediately sent it to the volunteer who helped me with the proposal. We celebrated together. I was so thankful for his help. We would not have received funding without his insider information or his willingness to volunteer his time for our cause.

The one-pager I mentioned above is a great resource for any organization, but is especially effective for smaller causes and individuals. This is also a great piece to send over by email as a follow-up to a phone conversation or an impromptu meeting. I always keep extra copies of the one-pager in my briefcase or bag that I keep in my car, and I make sure to have them with me at every meeting. You never know when you're going to run into a potential donor!

CREATE A CASE DOCUMENT

The case document is a great presentation piece to put together if you are asking for larger sums of money. A case document is necessary for a project campaign or capital campaign where you are asking potential donors for four, five, six, and seven-figure gifts to your organization. Your prospects will naturally want more details about a large project or campaign before making a decision to support your cause.

Imagine the process you would go through to purchase a bicycle versus a car. Purchasing a bike is a relatively large purchase, but the process is rather simple. You pick out the bike and you check out at the register. On the other hand, when you buy a car, the process isn't nearly as easy and there are a lot more emotions to the decision. Typically, you'd have to determine what kind of car you'd like, do your research online to compare your options, check the ads in the newspaper, window-shop at a dealership, test drive a few cars, and then make a decision as to what kind of car you want to buy and from whom you want to buy it from.

Think about your case document for those donors who are looking to invest a significant amount into your cause, like the purchase of a car. What will they need to know to make a decision? The case document should give your donors a clear idea on how their dollars will be spent, what solution your organization provides, and why your cause is the right fit for your supporter so they can make a decision to give.

I recommend an 11" x 17" booklet folded in the center, which gives you 8, 12, or 16 (8.5" x 11") pages of content, with the centerfold being your most important content.

Here's an example of how an 8-page case document may be laid out.

Page 1 – Front Cover: Design incorporating your logo and the date of the event/project.

Page 2 – Letter from the lead volunteer or executive director with an organizational timeline running across the bottom of pages 1 and 2.

Page 3 – An overview of your mission and/or organization, your event/project with details including who, what, when, where, and why.

Page 4 (center left) – Giving Opportunities

Page 5 (center right) – Giving Opportunities (cont.)

Page 6 – Results of your work and testimonials from other donors and individuals you serve.

Page 7 – How will you spend their dollars?

Page 8 – Back Cover: Design, mission statement, and contact information.

In addition to the case document, you'll need a response form that is a separate document or insert. The response form allows your donor to make a decision about their level of support for your event, project, or program. If you choose to include the form in your presentation piece, be sure the page is perforated and can be torn out of the packet to be completed and mailed or handed in during a meeting.

After completing the case document and response form, you'll want to present these materials in a professional presentation folder. Depending on the size of your campaign, a customized folder with your logo and design is a good investment. A basic folder purchased in bulk is a good alternative if you don't have the funds to get a customized piece. This allows for you to create a complete professional packet that can be customized for your prospect. The packet may include your presentation piece, your business card, your team leader's business card, and additional documents that may be relevant to the specific request you are making.

An important thing to remember is to pay attention to your print quality and how glossy your paper is. You want to be sure the response form can hold ink without smearing and your piece looks professional to your potential donors. This is also a document you want available in an electronic format. Ask your designer to provide you with a smaller file size document and a response form that can be completed and submitted online or by email.

Think through the options you have available to you to communicate with donors to make the process as simple as possible. The presentation piece is your opportunity to set the tone and introduce your brand in a clean presentation. Make it easy for your donor to say yes. Prior to completing the presentation packet, show the rough draft to your volunteer leader, and once again, give them the ability to share their feedback before you go to print. You want to be sure to confirm that you've made all the necessary edits, and your pictures, sponsorship or giving levels all make sense to the team.

CREATE A FUNDRAISING WEBSITE

Charity Navigator, an American independent charity watchdog organization, encourages donors interested in giving to go to the charity's website first, and if you still have questions, to go directly to a staff member. The most important thing for your charity to show on your website is that you are fulfilling your mission and you are getting positive results. The best place you can show your results is through your programs, accomplishments, goals, and challenges.

Your website should give you instant credibility and be the rallying point for all of your planning. It has to make a good first impression and be effective at getting people to take action.

In 2008, major United States television networks announced they were joining forces to host a telethon for the organization Stand Up 2 Cancer. Like many, I went to their website first. I wanted to know more about who they were and where their dollars were going. Was this organization credible? Their website answered my questions and confirmed they were credible. That year, they raised over $100 million in support of cancer research.

Your website should also be a quick and easy way to track down contact information for your organization. If someone sees your TV commercial, a billboard, or hear your radio ad, they should be able to find you by searching your name online. There will be times that you recruit volunteers or donors in unusual places. Your website allows a quick way for them to get plugged in to your cause.

There are many reasons why a website is important, including[6]:

- a warm introduction to show the community and potential volunteers and supporters who you are;
- recognition and introduction to your staff and volunteer leadership;
- a wealth of information;
- ability to take donations online and never have to interact face-to-face;
- be able to sell a fundraising product like t-shirts or promotional items;
- confirm their attendance for an upcoming event;
- invite them to be a volunteer and give volunteer opportunities;
- give the details for events on your organization's calendar;
- be an instant billboard or brochure available to anyone with a cell phone, tablet, or computer;
- 24-hour access for anyone, anywhere around the world;
- gives you a voice to say anything you want whenever you want; and
- instant contact information.

There are two different kinds of websites you may be interested in as a nonprofit leader: (1) an informational website with the ability to take donations, and/or (2) a fundraising website with the capacity to create fundraisers like birthday campaigns, walks, or 5k events.

An informational website includes your logo, possibly a promotional video, your mission statement, vision statement, staff and volunteer leadership, contact information, and a link to support the cause with a donation.

On the other hand, a fundraising site invites your guests to start a fundraising campaign for your organization. The primary use is for events or project campaigns and would include fundraiser specific information like the who, what, when, why, where, and how of your fundraiser.

On your home page you would give the viewer a way to start up a team or create a fundraising campaign for your cause. Many of these sites focus on birthdays or yearly events in communities around the country or world. You can pick the community you live in and immediately begin fundraising for the charity by sending out letters or emails to friends and family to support your campaign.

As you can see, you have a lot of control over how you present the look and feel of you and your organization. Regardless of whether you are new or a seasoned fundraiser, you can reinvent yourself at any time. It takes intention and focus back on your vision to ensure your message is coming across clear and of how you want to be perceived.

If you are not putting your best foot forward, now is the time to make a change. Start with your personal brand and work your way through to evaluate your logo, print materials, presentation, and website. If you have questions about how you are being perceived, don't be afraid to ask a group of supporters and volunteers to share their feedback through a survey or questionnaire.

CHAPTER 5

STEP 5: DEPLOY YOUR TEAM

"You choose how you show up to work: will you give it your best or just occupy space? This is also a choice for your team. Everyone is a volunteer. When you realize that, every person on your team becomes a gift. Your work as a leader shifts from force to invitation, from control to influence, from fear to gratitude."

– David Dye

The best team is a team where every member wants to be there. Over the course of the past two steps, you've enlisted your team and you've enhanced your brand. Now is the time to deploy your team and send them out into your community or target market to make an impact for your cause.

You've spent the time investing in them, and by this step, they should be properly trained with the skills needed to do the job. They have the professional materials to share with potential supporters, and they are educated on the vision, mission, and culture of your organization.

They are passionate and are empowered to share your message.

If you've done the previous steps well, your team will be made up of individuals who are bold and excited to spread your organization's message. They are wearing your logo and sharing information about your organization with pride.

Think of the largest employer in your community. It may be a hospital, school, or corporation. Imagine what the day-to-day activities look like for that group of people from the moment they start their workday until they leave at the end of their shift. When an employee started work at one of those places of employment, what sort of training do you think they went through? Did they receive an employee handbook? Do they understand the expectations of their specific position? Do they know the policies and procedures of the organization?

As a nonprofit organization grows just like a for-profit company, it is necessary to have an organized set of policies and procedures to keep the organization running. Your employees may need to go through an onboarding process to ensure every employee understands the culture and expectations of their new employer. This same process is so integral to the success of your organization when you grow and build your volunteer team.

Every member of your team should carry the responsibility of their department or job assignment just like the department head of any for-profit company. They should have a job description for their role and clear expectations to follow. By this step, you will realize that not everyone will be a good fit, but you've determined how to move unqualified team members to new positions and you're ready to deploy your "A" team.

VOLUNTEER AND STAFF PARTNERSHIP

Several years ago, a volunteer introduced me to the owner of a car dealership who had shown an interest in getting involved with our organization. I called him directly and scheduled a meeting with him to present our case document for our upcoming charity event. The lead volunteer and I walked into his office, and he shook both of our hands as we formally introduced ourselves.

He looked directly at my lead volunteer and said, "I'm genuinely interested. Why did you take the time to be here? You have a family and you don't get paid for this, right?" She immediately confirmed that she wasn't getting paid. She went on to share her story about how our organization had impacted her and her loved ones, and why she was passionate about making a difference. She wanted to stop the cycle and would do anything to ensure no one had to go through what her family and friends went through.

He was taken by her response. The fact that she would offer time out of her day to volunteer had impressed him. He was a businessman, and time meant money. She made it evident in her response that she felt her time was worth investing in our cause. Her request for him to make a donation was direct, and she was confident when she told him he wouldn't regret his decision to get involved. Needless to say, we left the meeting with a response form completed and signed with a commitment of support.

That meeting was a turning point for me and how I fundraise. I had been trained on the importance of the staff/volunteer partnership for years, but this meeting allowed me to see it firsthand.

During this meeting I had introduced myself and shared the impact of our organization, but my purpose for attending was as a resource only. That businessman didn't want to hear from another paid staff member from another charity in town telling him why his money was going to make a difference. He wanted to hear from an unbiased volunteer and donor who could tell him why he should care. The only person capable of doing that was another donor.

Take a moment and think about the last time a friend or family member told you about a great experience. Maybe it was a restaurant or maybe they bought a product they couldn't stop talking about. They were compelled to tell you about it because they had such a great experience. They went on to urge you to go to that restaurant or buy that product.

Word-of-mouth marketing is the best form of marketing hands down, and it's free. No one paid your friend or family member to tell you about their experience, but they couldn't help but tell you because they wanted to help you.

Now imagine it was the manager of the restaurant or the owner of the company telling you about the great experience you will have. How do you feel about their endorsement versus the endorsement of a friend or family member? Remember, that friend or family member has no skin in the game to say anything nice about their product or service. I'm sure you're thinking, "Of course, the manager or owner would say great things about their product or services."

When you enlist your team, you are looking for a team of people who are so passionate about your cause that they can't help but tell others about it. You are ultimately borrowing their platform to share you or your organization's story.

There are three ways to create a platform for your cause. You can (1) buy, (2) build, or (3) borrow your platform.

The issues with buying and building your platform is that buying your platform lacks credibility and costs you financially, and building it takes a lot of time. This is why your team is the secret to your success. The fact that your volunteer leader doesn't get paid makes them a credible and stronger voice for your organization.

Your team of volunteers should have strong influence with a diverse group of contacts, connections that would have taken you decades to build on your own. When your team grows from 1 to 10 to 50 to 100 members, you will see exponential growth of influence take place. It would be impractical to think that you could ever have the collective influence of your volunteer team. The best use of your time is to train, lead, and coach your team so they can be deployed to share your message to their circle of influence.

When those volunteers say yes to you or your organization, you now have the capacity to borrow their influence and credibility as they align themselves to you and your organization. If they are excited about the work you do, they will naturally want to tell others about it, just like the restaurant or the new gadget they bought.

The other thing to note is that high profile individuals with influence and strong credibility will never lend their name or align themselves with a poorly run organization. If they are passionate about the work you do and are bought in to your cause, it will be hard to pull them back from doing everything in their power to ensure your success. If their name is attached they won't allow you to fail, which also means they will feel compelled to ensure you run efficiently and that you see financial success.

Your organization's staff stories are not nearly as powerful as your volunteer's story. Your staff message may be clouded with desperation, depending on how dire the funds are needed. This may be your livelihood, and if you don't bring in new donors, it may put you and your family at risk.

Your volunteer team is your strongest sales force. If a volunteer will sacrifice their valuable time away from their career, family, or friends, how much greater will a potential donor be willing to sacrifice their hard earned money to support your organization.

TITLES ARE IMPORTANT

When you pick up the phone to make a call, I imagine you start by saying, "Hi, my name is" followed by your name, title, and important information to add credibility. If you are the CEO of XYZ Company, the fact that you are the CEO means you're in charge and you have influence. Your title gives you instant credibility and authority to speak with other high profile individuals at your level or below.

The same goes for titles within a nonprofit organization. Staff titles like CEO, founder, executive director, development director, or director of any kind will open the door to other decision makers. Your title tells the person on the other line that you have the authority to speak on behalf of your organization and with the organization's top leadership.

A title gives authority. If you are ready to deploy your team, your volunteers should be given the ability to speak on behalf of the organization with strong leadership titles. Your titles may include chair titles like event chairman, committee chairman, honorary chairman, board president, or advisory group chair.

If I said, "Hi John, this is Mary Valloni, Board President of the National Foundation," John should have an immediate understanding of what kind of position I hold within the organization and that I have decision-making power and influence.

If your volunteer is the chairman or chairwoman of a fundraising event, the honorary chair or a committee chair, there is a perceived value that they have some authority within your organization and they have a high level of authority when it comes to that specific event. We all want to feel like we are important. The same goes for corporate leadership. They don't want to waste their time with a low level volunteer if someone else in their organization can handle the call.

When a volunteer states their name and title and they have a personal relationship with someone within the company, there is a higher likelihood that they will be able to get a meeting scheduled with a company's decision maker. You never want to waste anyone's time—yours or theirs. If you can eliminate any concerns from their end by deploying a solid team, your success rate will increase significantly.

Your key volunteers are the most important members of the team. They are the voice, the face, and the army that represent you and your organization. You want the strongest and the most well trained force to be out in your community, the country, and the world, representing the work you do. By this stage, every volunteer carrying a title for your organization should have earned it. With the title comes respect and pride that they worked for the position they hold. That pride should speak loudly when they tell others.

When you assign a title, such as the president of the board of directors, it does not guarantee the person will feel a sense of pride. If you begged them to take the role, they will feel like they are doing you a favor. Watch your verbiage and the verbiage of your leadership team as they enlist the team. Be sure to set your standards high and use language that says this is an honor. You thought of them first for the position. If you set clear expectations, each member of your team will know how to hold each other accountable for the position they signed on to do.

If you and your team don't see your leadership positions as an honor for someone to fill, why would anyone else? You are creating a standard for your organization that best represents you and your vision. When you set a precedent for how your organization is run, it will affect all areas of your organization. If the bar is high when you enlisted your team, the bar will be high regarding expectations when it comes to results as you deploy your team.

VOLUNTEERS ARE DONORS

A study released by Fidelity Charitable Gift Fund and VolunteerMatch reported that 67% of Americans who volunteered in the past year say they "generally make their financial donations to the same organizations where they volunteer."

The study also reported "Americans who volunteer their time and skills to nonprofit organizations also donate an average of 10 times more money to charity than people who don't volunteer."

This tells me that (1) you need more volunteers, and (2) every one of your volunteers should be asked to give. Don't assume they should know or should feel obligated to give. You need to invite them the same way as you'd invite any other donor.

The volunteers who sell sponsorships and ask for donations should be donors themselves. If your most passionate volunteers are not willing to give a financial gift, why would anyone else give? Some may be dealing with a financial hardship and volunteering their time is all they can do in this season, but if they don't feel like your cause is worth giving to, you need to do your research and find out why.

It may not be that your cause isn't worthy of their gift; it may be that you missed the opportunity to ask them to give. Some volunteers who donate their time feel it's good enough to give their time and they don't "need" to donate financially as well. It is up to you to ensure that every prospect is asked, and that includes volunteers. This should be an easy ask.

Here is some verbiage to help you with the process. You might say, "Before we start inviting others to support our organization, we want to invite you to consider a gift. We don't want to miss the opportunity to invite you to financially support the mission."

It is extremely difficult to ask other people for money when you are not committed to the organization yourself. This is why I feel it is important to start by asking your volunteer team, who is about to go out and solicit funds, to first decide how they want to support your cause.

They have every right to decide not to give, but when you enlisted them for the team you went through a process to determine whether they were a good fit for their role. During the enlisting process, volunteers who are current or potential donors should have been at the top of your recruitment list. If you invested the appropriate amount of time in your volunteers to share your story, they should feel compelled to give.

The more informed you are about a cause, product, or service, the more likely you are to make the investment. If you have trained and educated your volunteers well they will feel compelled to give without being asked, but don't become complacent and miss out on the opportunity to invite them to donate. We'll talk more about making the ask in the next chapter.

In 2015, about 62.6 million people claimed to volunteer according to the U.S. Department of Labor, which means nearly 25% of the U.S. population volunteered somewhere. Most of those people were between the ages of 35 and 54, had a higher education, and volunteered with one or two organizations. Half of those who volunteered said someone asked them in the organization to get involved, and the other half said they approached the organization.[1]

I share this because I don't want you to lower your expectations of what your volunteers are capable of giving or doing for your organization. They can be skilled and wealthy individuals, and you can be selective and ask exactly who you want to be a part of your team. Don't be afraid to take the lead to ensure you have an elite group of volunteers and donors who are the best representatives for your organization.

LEAD YOUR VOLUNTEERS

Relationships are healthiest when there is a give and take. The same goes for the staff and volunteer partnership. When communication is strong and both parties feel like their voice is heard, they will be open to share their frustrations and roadblocks. This means you can talk through any situation and come up with a solution that works for everyone.

This is the difference between being a leader and micro-managing your volunteers. Everyone has a role to play, but each position is equally important. None of it will function properly if everyone isn't on the same page.

If you look at a car you may say the most important part of the car is the engine, while another may say the wheels are the most important. You can see that one doesn't work without the other. They are both equally important. The same goes for your team. Every member of the team has a responsibility to themselves, their teammates, and the organization to see to it that each job is done with excellence.

"Trust, but verify" was a statement used often by our 40th American President Ronald Reagan. He was taught the phrase as a means to communicate and work with the Soviet Union back in the 80's. When you enlisted your volunteers to work on a specific project, you trust that you trained them well, but you still need to verify they are capable of implementing the plan.

It takes time and practice to feel comfortable with the role you play in any organization. Imagine that it is like a learner's permit. You can drive, but someone else still needs to ride in the car. Those first couple of appoint-ments may be rough, but as time goes on they will feel more comfortable, and so will you. Everyone will begin to understand the value of each other's roles. The problem with many nonprofit leaders is that they are too busy to do the proper training, so they release the team too early with little supervision.

When I launched one of my fundraising events, I had a volunteer who was enlisted to help with the recruitment of other volunteers. He had just joined the committee, and within 48 hours of coming on board, I received a call from the marketing director of a large corporation in town. The human resources director knew me well enough to pick up the phone after she spoke with our newly recruited volunteer.

Our volunteer had called her company to ask for their involvement. That sounded good at first until she got into the part where he described the kind of volunteers we were looking to enlist. She went on to share that this gentleman described our event as so elite that we needed their employees, "the little people," to come and serve our elite guests.

My heart was in my stomach. "Our volunteer said what?" I asked. She repeated herself, and again I was sick. Somewhere along the line our story wasn't delivered well, and the last thing we wanted our volunteers to feel was *little*. Thankfully, I had a relationship with the director and she understood the miscommunication. She didn't hold this incident against us and I was able to have a conversation with the committee volunteer. She went on to say how she knew this didn't represent our organization and wanted to be sure we were aware of the situation.

Interactions like this made me very aware that there are a lot of moving parts as we build out a volunteer committee. You need to ensure that every volunteer who represents you and your organization's brand does so with the same level of excellence expected from the top-level leadership. Every member of the team is a reflection of your brand.

I realized it was my responsibility to ensure that everyone, regardless of their income, was welcome as a volunteer and donor to our organization. I needed to trust that every volunteer understood that, but I also knew it was imperative that I verify our message as coming across loud and clear. I wanted to ensure that by the time they were on their own this kind of situation would never happen again. Once again, this is why the vision and mission statements are so critical.

If you're going to be a volunteer-led organization, you want to give your volunteers room to learn and lead. It doesn't help anyone to hover and wait for a mistake. Empower them for the tasks ahead and give them a measure of legitimate freedom. You can go too far with this, of course, sacrificing your organization's vision by allowing too much flexibility. But don't let the fear of that extreme keep you from empowering your volunteers altogether.

VOLUNTEER OWNERSHIP

Just two years after we graduated college, my husband and I signed the paperwork on our first home in Missouri. It was one of those life-changing moments. The day we took ownership of that home I was so proud. Technically, the bank still owned the home, but we were homeowners.

In that moment it went from just "A" house to "OUR" house. When they handed us the keys, everything changed. Just like the keys to the house, we need to hand the keys to our organization over to our volunteers and give them ownership of our cause.

As soon as we change our vocabulary and start talking like "we" are in this together, "we" start coming up with ways to make a greater impact. We're willing to invite our friends and contacts because we don't want others to miss out on being a part of something so incredible.

Encouraging your volunteers to change their speech and inviting them to be insiders in your organization means that there is no longer an "us" and "them" mentality.

"Who" is your organization? Is it the building you are in? Your organization should be the people. The people of your organization have a mission to fulfill, and if you have a building, the building helps fulfill the mission but it is not the organization. You could get evicted out of your building and your cause would still exist. Your organization cannot be about you and your staff. It is so much bigger than that.

It takes everyone involved in your cause to make it all function. It takes your staff, your volunteers, the people you serve, and the donors who fund your mission. Everyone who makes up a part of your organization is the organization.

This just takes a little practice, but when you hear someone use the terminology that YOU should do something, it is so important that you stop them and correct the statement. "You mean WE should do something?" Your volunteers and donors will quickly get the hint that you can't do this alone.

If they want to see a change in your organization, you have to empower them to make it happen. If you want to feed the homeless or put shoes on kid's feet, let's figure it out and let's go do it! You'll see their eyes light up when you hand over the reins, and together you get to dream and come up with new ways to reach and serve your community to fulfill your mission.

If you use language that shows you are genuinely excited about your team's ideas, you will create a powerful team of people who know they can make a difference. You would never want to blow out their flame or ruin their enthusiasm for your cause. Just because it was done before doesn't mean it can't be done now.

Talk through your team's ideas and be honest about what may or may not work. Timing may allow you to make something work that hadn't in the past. Together you can achieve more, so keep the lines of communication open and encourage idea sharing.

Be sure to create an environment where there are no bad ideas. You should genuinely care about your team's thoughts and opinions. Not every idea is going to be a good one, but if you shoot down every idea, your volunteers, staff, and leaders will get the hint that their ideas are not welcome and they'll stop sharing them with you.

CHAPTER 6
STEP 6: ORGANIZE YOUR ASK

The fall of 1999, I entered my sophomore year of college as a transfer student. I loved high school and I dreaded the thought of missing one moment of my senior year to do research on colleges. So during my freshman year at the University of North Dakota, I focused my vision, ran my research, and landed at Southwest Missouri State University (now Missouri State University) in Springfield, MO.

It was only a few weeks into the school year before I met my husband. The first time I saw him was at a weeknight bible study in the ballroom of the university student union. He was playing the drums. When the music ended, he ran across the room and jumped on the back of a guy with a stronger build who stood at least a foot taller than him.

He was extremely energetic, loud, and appeared to enjoy the attention. That day we passed by each other and remained strangers for weeks, but today, he is the single most important person in my life.

There are a lot of people in this world who are strangers to your organization today. They may not know how or why they should be a part of your team, but that doesn't mean that one-day they couldn't be your strongest supporter.

My husband was a stranger in August—we met in September—and he became my boyfriend in October. A year later, we were engaged. Two years later, we were married, and we just celebrated our fifteenth anniversary. Your volunteers may be strangers today, but in a few weeks or months you could enlist and deploy them. Within no time they could be supporting and representing your cause, passionate about making a difference.

DATING VS. FUNDRAISING

Looking at the fundraising process through the lens of dating can be extremely effective. You may be so anxious to ask someone to give to your cause because you can see how great you can be together, but remember, you are strangers. You don't want to be a stalker or come on too strong. Can you imagine asking for someone's hand in marriage the first time you meet? Sadly, this happens in fundraising way too often when we ask for a donation during our first meeting.

Let's look at the dating and fundraising process side by side. Notice that you'll never find a date or a donor to your cause if you don't first find out where they hang out. If you want to date a particular type of guy or girl, you first have to find out where the best place is to meet. The same goes for your donor or volunteer prospects. You want to identify whether you are a good fit first before you take the time to get to know them.

Here are the typical steps to dating:

- Determine what you want in a partner (vision and research)
- Strangers meet for the first time (introduced by a friend, family member, or you introduce yourself)
- Small talk
- Exchange phone numbers or contact information
- Schedule a first date
- Get to know each other
- Determine if you like each other and have similar interests
- Go on a second date

- Start communicating more frequently
- Share openly about why you like each other (gifts, compliments, acts, hold hands)
- Proposal or engagement
- Long-term commitment (marriage)

Here are the steps to the fundraising (sales) process:

- Determine your ideal donor (vision and research)
- Create a prospect list and figure out how you can meet
- Ask for an introduction from a friend or acquaintance
- Exchange or acquire contact information
- Make contact with the prospect
- Schedule a first meeting (coffee or lunch)
- Qualify if they are interested in your cause and what specific areas they'd like to support
- Schedule a second meeting
- Present your proposal and ask for their support
- They give you a gift of time, money, product, or service
- You respond with a thank-you gift, recognition, appreciation, handshake/hug
- Long-term commitment to your cause

In both situations, each future partnership starts out with two strangers but ends in a relationship that becomes long term. If you want larger gifts for your organization, you will need to spend more time and engage your donors in a relationship. Here are some examples of how organizations have taken donors who give smaller gifts to six- and seven-figure gifts.

Holding Hands

Gifts of $25 or less: May include a bake sale, car wash, or the Salvation Army Red Kettle. This level of donation requires little commitment from the organization and the donor.

The First Date

Gifts of $50 - $100+: First time gifts or donations to an email or viral campaign like a walk or online challenge. You are starting to build trust.

In a Relationship

Gifts of $1,000+: This may include sponsorship donations or monthly giving of $75 or more a month. The donor believes in you and your mission, and they are interested in giving to your cause monthly or yearly.

Part of the Family

Gifts of $10,000+: This includes larger sponsorships and lead gifts for your organization. At this level, it is as if you have invited them to be a part of the family. They feel connected to you and are connected to others within your organization.

Long-term Commitment

Gifts of $100,000+: Your donor is now looking at large projects that will change the face of your organization. This is often seen as legacy giving or gifts that come from wealthy donors. Donors with more disposable income will typically lean toward large gifts instead of monthly giving. Note that high dollar donors will not make payments on a house if they can buy the house.

In this relationship, your values strongly align and they see the long-term benefits their gift could make on your organization.

Long-term Commitment (Anniversary, Special Occasions)

Gifts of $1 million+: This opportunity may come about with a capital campaign or large one-time project. Your donor may have won the lottery, sold a business, or received an inheritance. To be ready for gifts of this size, your organization must have a vision large enough to receive and utilize large donations. You and your donor do not want to destroy the work you have done or ruin the relationship by giving you a gift you are not prepared to receive. If your vision is a million-dollar vision, start planning out what this could look like so you attract donors of this size.

THE POWER OF MONEY

Asking for help in the form of money is hard for a lot of people. It brings up insecurities, fear, and self-doubt. You may be afraid of rejection, or making someone feel uncomfortable or offended. You may even feel like you are begging or asking them to pay your bills.

Donors typically don't want to feel like they are paying your bills, but they do understand that bills need to be paid to fulfill your mission. Ultimately, donors want to be invited to be a part of your mission. There will be people who want to know the details about every line item of your budget, but for the most part, people give because it feels good to give and they want to make a difference.

A common statement I hear is that male fundraisers believe females have an easier time with the ask, and females often believe men have the advantage. I don't believe there is a superior gender when it comes to fund-raising. I do believe the most successful fundraisers are the ones who are the most confident. They are convinced they are making a difference, and they are excited to share their story and invite others to be a part of it. A strong fundraiser has confidence in their abilities, but is strong enough to understand that they cannot do it alone.

That confidence will grow within you as you walk through the seven steps. Too often, nonprofit leaders jump right to this step and start asking everyone and anyone for money. Your donors will respond differently if they feel like they received a special invitation to be a part of your cause rather than just being another name on your list.

If you send out a mass mailing, you may be able to tap into the first date level of a relationship, but you will need a plan and multiple interactions to move them from the dating phase to bringing them into the family. We all know that we'll part with a few dollars on just about anything, but we won't part with larger donations without a personal investment and a relationship of some sort with the organization.

That relationship could come quickly or could take years to build and nurture. This goes back to why I believe volunteers are the best at making the ask because you can borrow their platform and avoid years of relationship building. No matter how great your cause is, you still need the stories and testimonials from your constituents, volunteers, and donors to show you are making a difference. Otherwise, you're just another good cause that is probably doing good work but is underfunded and functioning in a place of desperation.

Dave Ramsey, an expert in personal money management, challenges people to change their thoughts around money. He reminds them that money is amoral. Money doesn't have guiding principles of its own and money won't change who you already are.[1]

When we or our organizations bring in more money, it just makes us more of who we already are. If you are a generous person and you get wealthy, you become a generous, wealthy person, but if you are a poor, greedy jerk and you get wealthy, you're probably going to be a rich, greedy jerk. It's all about whose hands the money is in, not about the money itself.

Dave shares how money is like a brick. In the hands of the right person, a brick can be used to build a home or office building, but in the hands of the wrong person it can be used to break your car window to steal your wallet.

This analogy gives us a very practical comparison. We give money way too much power and value. It is just a thing, yet just like addicts, you can turn an object like money, drugs, shopping, and alcohol into an obsession.

Before you ask your donors for money, it is a good thing for you to understand what kind of value you are personally giving to money.

Is money just a tool or are you giving it more power than that? Money should not be the goal, mission, or vision of the work you do. I chuckle at the thought of an architect giving a brick the same kind of value we as individuals, fundraisers, or nonprofit leaders give to money.

How much money is enough? How many bricks will it take to run and maintain your organization? Many organizations automatically assume that more is better and nothing is ever good enough. We assume that with more money we can do more good, but that is not always the case.

If you don't have a clear vision of what your organization is here on earth to do, you will sell out to the highest bidder. Your organization should be worth more than a check. Turning down a check is hard to do, but when money is amoral and just a thing, it becomes a lot easier to stay focused on your vision without compromise.

Setting a base level fundraising goal will also keep you and your organization away from burnout. We talked about that in Step 3. The last thing you want is to feel like it's never good enough. There's got to be a dollar amount that is good enough, and when you go above and beyond that level, you celebrate by funding new programs and projects on your wish list. It is unrealistic to think that your organization will see an increase in funding every year and not take into consideration the ups and downs that are bound to occur.

WHO YOU SHOULD ASK

We've spent a lot of time talking about building relation-ships with volunteers and donors because of the impact individuals have on giving. Individuals make up 71% of all giving, but rationally, it was an individual who made the decision for 100% of all giving. An individual made the decision for gifts made from a foundation, bequests, and corporate giving. Without individual giving, our charities wouldn't exist. We need each other and we are naturally wired with the desire to support each other.

According to Giving USA Foundation, Americans had another record setting year with donations reaching $373.25 billion in 2015 going to the following organizations[2]:

- 33% ($119.3 billion) to religion
- 16% ($57.48 billion) to education
- 12% ($45.21 billion) to human services
- 11% ($42.26 billion) to gifts to foundations
- 8% ($29.81 billion) to health
- 7% ($26.95 billion) to public-society benefit
- 5% ($17.07 billion) to arts, culture, and humanities
- 4% ($15.75 billion) to international affairs
- 3% ($10.68 billion) to environment and animals
- 2% ($6.56 billion) to gifts to individuals

This information is interesting, not only to see the per-centage breakdown but to see the dollar amount as well. I often hear from fundraisers, "No one wants to give to my charity. We aren't curing cancer, saving babies, or helping puppies." Based on these statistics, cancer, babies, and puppies aren't even at the top of the list.

Individuals give the most to religious organizations and schools, which is no surprise. These organizations have the ability to build relationships and create deeper roots. The average individual giving to a religious organization will typically participate in a weekly gathering. They know the leadership by name and they build relationships as if they were a part of the family. They may share meals together, celebrate birthdays, weddings, the birth of children, and walk with each other through tragedies and death.

Those who give to educational institutions may have personally attended the school or university they support for four years or more. The donor may have been a recipient of a previous donation to the institution. Their children may have or are currently attending the school. Many see investing in the lives of children as investing in our future.

Once again, it's all about relationship. The millions of causes in our world are important, but we only have the ability to support a handful of them in a lifetime. You don't need to invite all of them to support your cause; you just need to find the ones who align with your vision and mission that you can welcome into the family and partner together for a longer period of time.

ASK FOR PRODUCTS OR SERVICES

There are two types of donations that can be given to a nonprofit organization. The first is cash and the second is an in-kind donation of an asset, often a product or a service. I encourage you to make a list of all the products and services you are currently paying cash for and see if you can align yourself with a company or individual who would be interested in covering that expense.

In-kind donations are often an easier request or ask. Imagine if someone knocked on your door and asked for a cup of sugar. You'd probably go right to your pantry and wouldn't think anything of it. Of course you'd give a cup of sugar, flour, milk, or a couple of eggs to your neighbor who is in need.

Now imagine that same neighbor knocking on your door asking if you'd give them a couple of dollars to buy the sugar, flour, milk, or eggs. Your giving attitude may have just changed. Now they want cash. Really? What do they need my dollars for?

We don't place near as much value on products and services. It may be because you, the organization or the corporation, has already purchased the product and no longer has the attachment to it because it is no longer in cash form. This is where you can use in-kind donations to your advantage to eliminate your expenses.

You may think that no one would part with the things you need. You'd be surprised at what people will donate. A little time and energy could go a long way in making the request for in-kind donations. If you start by eliminating your expenses, you will ultimately need less cash on the income side. You either have an income problem or an expense problem. They are equally important to fulfilling your budget.

There are many reasons why in-kind donations are worth your time. Look at the budget you created in Step 1 and highlight the budgeted products and services throughout your expense list.

Are you paying for your event facility, food, drinks, decorations, rental equipment, stage, sound, lights, and hotel rooms for speakers or entertainers? How about non-event related expenses like office rental space, storage space, transportation or the purchase of a van or shuttle, printing expenses, office supplies, office furniture, phones, utilities, web hosting and design? If you are raising a personal budget you may see items like groceries, utilities, medical expenses, travel expenses, a home, car, cell phone, and a computer on your list.

If you take a good look at your budget you may see that a good portion of your income going out is to pay for products and services. Now some organizations need more cash donations due to salaried employees, or the actual purpose of the organization is to give financial support back to the community. But for those of you distributing product, what if you could eliminate your expenses by partnering with in-kind contributors so you have less need for cash? Put together a list of companies that could potentially donate to a line item expense through the donation of a product or service.

ASK CORPORATIONS OR ORGANIZATIONS

So you've exhausted all your options for in-kind donations and it is time to ask for the cold hard cash. My philosophy is, "They are going to give it to someone. It might as well be you!"

Realize that not every dollar is created equal. There are dollars that you manage and there are dollars that you earn. Obviously, the dollars that you manage are easier to part with because there is less emotional attachment to the money. When you look at corporate or organizational dollars, there will be individuals within their team who are responsible for determining how to spend their budgeted line items for charitable contributions and marketing dollars.

There are typically two buckets of money here: charitable giving and marketing. The managers of these two buckets are no different than the office managers who determine how many paper clips your office should have at any one given time. When you need it, you buy it. That same level of attachment is there for the employee who oversees an organization's charitable donations and marketing dollars.

If you can show that they need you, like they need paperclips, they'll pay attention and will consider partnering with you. There is less emotion attached to the dollars here. They are going to spend those dollars somewhere; they might as well spend them with you!

So the big question is, how do I get in their budget? There are many ways to get in an organization's budget. Once again, this is why organizing and making the ask is Step 6 and not Step 1. Throughout the past 5 steps you have focused your vision, run your research, enlisted your team, enhanced your brand, and deployed your team.

You should know by this stage whether this company or organization is a good fit because they align with your values, they have the ability to give, you have enlisted a volunteer team member to your organization that has a relationship with their organization, you've pulled together presentation materials that appeal to the decision maker, and your volunteer has scheduled a meeting. The ask is inevitable, and by this stage, your team is confident that this organization is a good fit for you and for them. You are the paperclip they need.

Many organizations encourage their employees to give back and serve somewhere in the community. If you did your research right, you know exactly who those organizations are and you targeted their employees when you enlisted your team. This is why every step of the process is important.

As new information about a company becomes available, you can always go back and add new members to your team. For instance, you may not have realized their policy is to only support causes their employees support. Go back to Step 3 and enlist a team member from their company to your team. Don't be afraid to ask for a volunteer nomination if you have a relationship with someone in the company's leadership. Their nomination could help you avoid unnecessary research and may encourage the volunteer to say yes when you ask.

On your first visit with the company or organization you may have gotten a no. Don't freak out! The great thing about the meeting is that you are gaining valuable information. This meeting will now be turned into part of your research, and you are back to Step 2. Put the company on your wish list or prospect list to recruit a volunteer from their company. Walk that volunteer through the process, and in six months or a year, you'll be ready to go back and approach the organization again for funds.

You'll be surprised at how quickly the conversation turns around. Remember, they want to partner with organizations that are a good fit. You have to decide whether it is worth your time and energy to get in alignment with their process to be a good fit and be considered for funding.

Other ways you can receive corporate funds is through company grants and matching donations. This is a great way to receive funding and to potentially double your donations. If an employer provides a matching donations program, every dollar donated by their employees is matched dollar for dollar with corporate funds.

Another common employee program encouraging volunteerism is a company that donates their employee's hourly wage or a set dollar amount for every hour their employees volunteer with your organization. Yes, they will pay you, and their employees will volunteer their time to work for you for free! You just have to do your research to learn what companies offer these programs in your community, and then be willing to do the work to go get the funds.

ASK INDIVIDUALS

The most common source of donations is through individuals who have earned their income. They still manage their funds like an employee manages corporate funds, but this is a different ball game. These are the donations that were earned. The fist tends to be tighter on these funds, and your relationship to the individual and their family must be stronger.

In 2015, the average annual household contribution was $2,974[3] with 98.4% of high net worth households giving to charity.[4] That percentage is important. High net worth individuals want to give, and 63% of them cite "giving back to the community" as their chief motivation for giving.[5]

The greatest percentage of high net worth households gave to educational (85%) and basic needs (81%) organizations, followed by 70% to the arts, 67% to health-related organizations, and 67% to religious organizations.[6]

Regardless of whether an individual is high net worth or low net worth, building relationships with individuals is crucial. They have the ability to make one-time gifts, monthly gifts, and annual gifts to you and your organization. Their giving can withstand life changes like a change in a job, a move, children, or a death in the family. If you have a strong relationship, the partnership will last through the ups and downs of life.

ASK FAMILY OR FRIENDS

This can be the easiest or the hardest ask to make out of the list. Asking a family member or close friend can be the easiest because they know you and love you, and it can be the hardest because they know you and love you. If you come from a family or circle of friends who are impacted and are just as passionate about your mission as you are, they should definitely be on your prospect list.

If your family and friends have never shown an interest in the area of your mission, I would recommend that you don't put them at the top of your prospect list just because they know and love you. Your research in Step 2 should have shown you whether or not they were a good fit for you or your organization.

This is a tricky group of people to target because you can easily turn into the family member or friend who is selling Tupperware, Mary Kay, or any other multi-level marketing product. Not that any of those are bad, but when you start looking at your family as customers instead of family it can ruin or change the relationship.

I don't want to see your fundraising turn into a Tupperware party. Your mission is way too important for it to be a burden on you or anyone else. Because of the passion you have for what you do, you'll naturally share with them what you're doing and possibly your fundraising-dollar goal. If your family or friends show an interest and want to support you, that is great, but don't set expectations that they have to or you'll be hurt or upset.

I just want to be sure you are sensitive with this category. Remember, these are the people you love the most. The last thing you want to see happen is that you show up to Thanksgiving dinner and all your supporters are sitting around the table. Your dinner won't taste the same.

The other thing to consider is that you work Monday through Friday and often nights and weekends. Wouldn't it be nice to go home and spend time with your family without thinking about "work"? Some of you have missions that take over every facet of your life, but sometimes you just want to spend time with mom and dad or grandma without expectations of anyone owing each other anything.

For most of my fundraising career, my closest friends and family lived relatively far away so this wasn't an issue, but when we moved closer to family they wanted to help out. I never hesitated to invite them in, but I recall the first family gathering where I spent my entire afternoon responding to questions about our upcoming fundraiser.

One family member, who was the most excited about getting involved, started asking other family members to donate as well. I could see she was putting the others in a difficult situation where they felt obligated to say yes because they didn't want to let "me" down. Even though I wasn't the one asking, they still felt the pressure to help me out.

You may also have a situation where not every family member will be supportive. Asking for money brings up a lot of emotions, depending on your family's upbringing. It may be a cultural issue or it may be that your family doesn't agree with the mission of your organization. Just because this is your calling doesn't mean it should be theirs.

I personally react poorly to direct marketing from family and friends, and sadly, I've lost friends over it. I don't like feeling pressured or be expected to donate purely because we are family or friends. The last thing I want to do is put my family and friends in a position where they feel trapped or be in a high-pressured situation to give.

Even if they say yes, these individuals will be the first ones to abandon your cause the moment you give them a way out. If you leave your organization for any reason, they are likely to stop their donations to that cause as well.

There is little sustainability for your organization with this approach unless your family and friends become passionate about the cause. The challenge to this approach is overcoming the donor's loyalty to you as an individual and little to no loyalty to your overall organization. If you educate them enough on the impact of your organization's mission and they get to know others within your organization, you can increase the odds that they will continue their involvement whether you are there or not. I believe you will have stronger supporters if they are aligned with the mission without obligation to a single individual within the organization.

ASK A STRANGER (COLD CALLING)

This is often seen as the least effective approach to fundraising, but still an approach that is worth your time. If you've done your homework and walked through all the previous steps, cold calling won't be necessary.

When you created your prospect list, you put together names on your list that you may or may not have known at the time. After running your research and enlisting your team, you should now have access to the names on your list through your team members so your calls are rarely cold calls.

If you find yourself in a position where the only option is to cold call the individual or company, I suggest you take the "Can you help me approach." We are all much more receptive when someone on the other end of the phone asks for our help, especially from the person who answers the phone.

The receptionist's primary job is typically customer service. If you ask for help, they will naturally feel compassionate to do all they can to help you. That and you avoid coming off as aggressive. If you take a friendly approach and are genuinely interested in their help, they will hear that in your voice and will want to help you.

The question may be, "Hi, my name is (NAME) and I was wondering if you could help me. I'm trying to reach the person who handles your charitable contributions."

From there, the individual on the phone will self-identify the right person for you to talk with. If you are calling in regards to a product or service, say for an auction item, this will be a common call they are used to receiving and will share their process with you to make your request. If you are looking to meet with someone in a special department, you'll want to address the need you are looking to fill.

In any circumstance, be sure to see your request from the perspective of the individual on the other end. Would you want to help you?

Organizing the ask is the step that will bring in all the donations to your organization. If you are not organized and you haven't thought through the details, your budget will reflect it. This should be a fun process and extremely rewarding. Take each step seriously and it will be hard for your donors to say no. You should see great success if you've taken the time to do the previous steps. When you make the ask you will feel a sense of accomplishment and confidence that you got this!

CHAPTER 7

STEP 7: MAKE YOUR DIFFERENCE

Congratulations! You made it to the final step, and because of your hard work and planning your donor said YES! You've just completed your event or individual ask, and you're raising the funds you need to fulfill your mission. You've made it to Step 7 and it is time to make your difference and CELEBRATE your success!

This should be the "fun step," but you'd be surprised at how many will skip the celebration all together. Most will jump right back to Step 6 to ask for more money. This is the time to stop and reflect on the work that went into the process, thank your new donors, and celebrate with your team all that you have accomplished.

Besides showing appreciation to your new donors, it is also time to ensure your team knows how much they are appreciated and valued. This is what you've worked so hard to achieve. You now have the ability to fulfill the vision and mission of your organization. What can you do now that you've raised the funds? Be sure to share the results with your team and celebrate together.

Here's what you don't want to happen. Imagine someone asked you for help and you graciously helped them out, but then moments later, they turned around and asked again before they even thanked you for the last time you helped them. What would be your immediate reaction?

You may think they are ungrateful, rude, and self-centered, and you may start to think that this is a one-sided relationship. You don't want you or your organization to be perceived as being any of those things. By the time you reach this step, you've grown together as a team and you should genuinely care about each of your team members and donors who've made an investment of time, money, or resources to your cause.

You want every member of your team to feel appreciated and loved and wanting to come back. The goal would be that they not only come back, but that they come back stronger year after year and continue to increase their investment of time and support to your cause. Even if your fundraising goal isn't met, ensure your volunteers and donors don't feel as though their efforts were a failure.

After you've collected and confirmed that the donations are in the bank, it's time for you, your staff, volunteers, and donors to celebrate. Each situation will be unique. If this is an individual gift, you will celebrate with that individual in a different way than if you have a group of supporters all investing through an event. We'll dig deeper into each scenario and discuss how to sustain your staff, volunteers, and donors, and how to win them over year after year.

SPEAK YOUR TEAM'S LANGUAGE

When my husband and I got married, we received a book called *5 Love Languages* by Gary Chapman. This book was eye opening not only in my marriage, but also with the relationships in my life including volunteers and donors. In the book, Gary explained that we each have a "love tank" that must be filled to fulfill our need to be loved. The love languages include: gifts, quality time, words of affirmation, acts of service, and physical touch.[1]

You can take Gary's quiz on 5lovelanguages.com to identify your love language to help you better understand how you give and receive love. My love language is quality time. Early on in my marriage, I would be disappointed when my husband was working out of our home office. The day we purchased a laptop and he started working from the living room, I saw an immediate change in my love tank. It made all the difference to just have him in the same room, which equated to spending more quality time together. It seems silly, but small gestures like being in the same room together can make a big difference.

Realizing how powerful the love languages are, I became more aware of how I could use them to identify the love languages of my volunteers and donors. I spent the most time with my volunteer team. When I became aware of the love languages, I saw how my volunteers were looking to fill their love tank through their volunteer work. I quickly realized that I wasn't very good at implementing all five of the love languages to show my appreciation to the team. What I did notice was that I had a tendency to lean on my own dominant love languages, which were quality time, words of affirmation, and physical touch.

You may think your love language is obvious, but it may be beneficial to take the quiz to figure it out. To some degree we enjoy all five areas, but definitely to varying degrees, and we don't naturally have the ability to enjoy all the love languages to the extent that they fill our love tank.

Your volunteers and donors will give you hints as to what their language is, but you have to be willing and able to pick up on their cues. If someone says they don't like public recognition, it is critical that you don't force them to get up on stage to receive an award or a special thank-you.

Others will make reference to their disappointment in organizations that spend their donations on gifts. Don't miss an opportunity to recognize your team members in the way that is most appropriate for each individual, and find a way to incorporate all five love languages into your stewardship plan.

Here's how you can implement the five love languages.

1. Receiving Gifts
   - Give promotional items with your logo prominently displayed (T-shirts, jackets, mugs, pens, notebooks, journal, motivational book, etc.)
   - Awards and trophies
   - Thank-you cards
   - Flowers
   - Special occasion gifts (holidays, birthday, anniversary, baby, etc.)

2. Quality time (giving undivided attention)
   - One-on-one meetings
   - Committee meetings
   - Lunch or group gatherings
   - Being attentive during each conversation (no distractions or multi-tasking)

- Set aside volunteer workspace in your office so you have more time together

3. Words of Affirmation (using words to affirm other's actions)
   - Confirmation that you need them and appreciate their involvement
   - Verbal thank you
   - Reassurance they are doing a great job
   - Phone calls, text, and social media message complimenting them for the work they are doing or referencing a personal situation where you are thinking of them.
   - You value their opinion and verbally share their contributions publicly with your team

4. Acts of Service (actions speak louder than words)
   - Offer to help with their volunteer area to ensure they are successful
   - Order or purchase materials they have recommended
   - Share updates when they cannot attend a group gathering or meeting, and share minutes to the meeting so they don't miss out on important information
   - Ensure their area is seen as important and integral to the success of your organization
   - Go out of your way to help during a personal time of need

5. Physical Touch
   - Handshakes
   - High fives or fist bumps
   - Hugs
   - Patting on the shoulder or back

A few years ago, my lead volunteer made a connection with a woman who was interested in donating to our auction. She went through her antique collection and donated several pieces of jewelry. She clearly took a lot of pride in each piece as they were labeled with great detail.

One day while she was visiting in the office, I made a reference to one of the pieces she donated. I shared that I really liked a particular ring she put in the auction. We joked about how I'll have to have my husband get over to the auction and be sure to bid on it for me. I really liked the ring, but in my mind I was giving her words of affirmation on how I appreciated her generosity to the cause and her willingness to donate to our organization.

The week following the event, she stopped by the office unexpectedly and was anxious to hear how the fundraiser went and how well the auction did. She immediately asked if I was able to bid on the ring we previously talked about. Of course I was extremely busy the night of the event, and as a staff member, I didn't bid on the auction items.

She seemed so disappointed that I didn't get the ring and shared how she had another one just like it. I tried to reassure her that it was more than okay that I hadn't gotten the piece and that the gentleman who got it was very excited when he picked it up.

A few days later, she was back at the office and in her hand was a gift. She was smiling from ear to ear, and she was so happy to bring with her an almost near identical ring to the original piece. She handed it to me and said, "It's for you! I want you to have it."

I was flattered by her generosity, but our policy was to not accept gifts from volunteers and donors. I tried to explain to her that I couldn't receive it, but she insisted that I keep it. I shook my head and just smiled, thanking her for thinking of me and wanting me to have the gift.

She left, and I went back to my work wrapping up the event and finalizing gifts to our sponsors, writing thank-you cards, ensuring auction items got to our guests, and that all the money had gotten in the bank. I didn't think much more of the gift as I went on with my work.

A few months later I was asked to represent our organization at a community fair. I had taken the morning shift and I came in early to set up our booth. Throughout the morning I shared information about our organization with those who stopped by the booth.

I was about two hours into my three-hour shift when a woman approached me at the booth. I didn't recognize her at first, but after a few moments I was able to connect how we knew each other. I smiled and reached across the table to give her a hug and asked her how'd she been. She cut me off before I got very far. Her tone was no longer positive and she began to talk to me in a firm and aggressive voice.

She started by sharing how she went out of her way to come to my office to bring me a gift and how disrespectful it was that I had not sent her a personalized thank-you card to show my appreciation for the ring she gave me. I thought to myself how I had sent her a thank-you card, but realized that it was directed toward her donation to the organization and not specifically for the personal gift.

She went on to say how she wanted this to be a "teachable moment" for me. In the moment, I was so hurt. I love the work I do and my desire is to ensure that every donor and volunteer knows they are appreciated. My heart was broken to think that she was that upset with me because of a thank-you card.

As soon as she walked away from the booth, tears flooded my eyes and I couldn't control them. I was shaking and I had to immediately remove myself from the booth. My co-worker, who was standing near me, saw the woman approach the table but didn't hear our conversation. She saw that I was visibly upset and asked if I was okay. I couldn't hold it together. I've worked with thousands and thousands of people but never had someone talk to me that way.

The woman was also a contact of my lead volunteer, and all I could think of was how I had upset her and how this could impact the relationship with my event chairman. As soon as I pulled myself together, I called that volunteer to share what had happened and to apologize for my oversight.

Thankfully, my volunteer was very compassionate and consoled me, reassuring me that I hadn't done anything wrong. After processing the situation, I realized I had completely disregarded the woman's love language of gift giving. I should have known. The signs were all there. She gave me a gift, which was her love language, and I gave her words of affirmation, a verbal *thank you*, and physical touch, a hug, which were my love languages. Reflecting back, I can see how we both genuinely cared, but we didn't know how to effectively communicate with each other.

Appreciation can be misinterpreted as easily as that. I never anticipated I'd find myself in that position where I clearly had upset a donor and she clearly had upset me. The love languages show us that our volunteers and donors are not the same, nor should they be treated as such. Be sure to thank your volunteers and donors using their appropriate love language, and to avoid any potential miscommunication, consider utilizing all five languages in your future plans.

CREATE A THANK YOU PLAN

Before you can celebrate an individual supporter, reflect back on Step 2 when you ran your research. You should have identified key details about each of your donors and volunteers. Pay attention to the details about their lives. The information they share will give you key information as to how they want to be thanked. Creating a donor stewardship or "thank you" plan ensures that donors don't slip through the cracks.

A general rule of thumb is to follow the Chinese custom of thanking donors a minimum of seven times[2]. Here is an example of what your seven thank yous may look like. Please be sure to customize these to best connect with your donor and utilize their love language if possible.

Thank You 1. If a financial gift is made online, an automated email response should go out to your donor to confirm their donation and thank them for their gift. If a check was mailed in, a quick phone call within three days from a staff member to notify them that their check was received, especially if this was a large gift. You don't want your donor to wonder if their donation ever got to your organization. This eases their mind and shows them that you are organized and you value their gift.

Thank You 2. Immediately after receiving a donor's gift, send a brief handwritten thank-you card from the volunteer/staff who has the relationship with the donor. This is a must. Sit down and take a few minutes to put into words what their donation has allowed your organization to do. All donations, no matter the size, should receive an immediate thank you. Depending on your relationship with the donor, the medium of that communication may differ.

This goes back to knowing your donor. If you commonly communicate by email, social media, or text, continue to use that medium to immediately respond with excitement and enthusiasm of their support, but follow it up with a written thank you as well. Depending on the level of support, it may be appropriate to consider sending a small commemorative gift as well.

I had an individual respond to my confirmation of support by sending me an email that read he was literally doing the happy dance in his living room. That made me so happy. That simple comment made an immediate impression on me as a donor. He expressed excitement and enthusiasm, and in that moment, I knew I wasn't just another donor. He reminded me that my donation mattered. Don't underestimate the value of sharing that excitement with your donor.

Thank You 3. A phone call or personal letter from the CEO/Executive Director/Leadership within 30 days of receiving the donation. This personal call or letter from your leadership shows that all levels of your organization care. It tells your donor they have access to your leadership and they matter not only to you but to the leadership as well. I encourage you to establish a minimum gift amount here (i.e. $500, $1k, $5k, $10k) that warrants a call or letter from your leadership to ensure your Executive Director is not overwhelmed with phone calls.

Thank You 4. A letter from your board of directors or your board chairman (if you have a board). Once again, acknowledgement from your leadership shows you are organized and you care at all levels of your organization.

Thank You 5. A brief thank-you card or letter from your lead volunteer. If this was an event, this thank you may go out from the event chairman, a sub-committee chairman, or a volunteer who oversaw a specific area of the event. A thank you from a non-paid volunteer or an individual that you serve will go a long way with your donors.

Thank You 6. Recognize your donor in your annual report or another organizational publication. You may have a monthly, quarterly, bi-annual, or annual news-letter that goes out to all your donors and prospective donors. This is a great way to thank your donor with name recognition or highlight their support in a brief article.

Thank You 7. Recognizing your donor at an upcoming event or banquet is a great way to acknowledge their contribution. Donor events come in all shapes and sizes. Once again, know your audience. This may be hosted in a home, on site at a facility they funded, in your office building, a banquet hall, a sponsor's business, etc. It may be a kickoff to the next fiscal year, or be hosted in conjunction with a big announcement or grand total of your most recent fundraising event.

Thank You 8. I know I said seven, but the eighth thank you is critical. This is the thank you before you ask again. Be sure to acknowledge a donor's past contributions before your next ask.

I encourage you to customize the plan for each relationship. With the addition of social media, you should know how to best connect so they know they matter to you and your organization. Remember, they have a choice to give or not to give to your cause. Don't give them any reason not to give.

There will be a time where you encounter a donor that you just can't please. In those moments, just do your best and then let it go. Be confident that you did everything in your control to show your appreciation. This donor may feel that you don't appreciate their dollars as much as they do.

They worked hard for the money they've made, and it is difficult to meet everyone's expectations. Do your best to create an environment where your donors feel good about giving to your cause. Some people are natural givers and others are not. It's not easy for everyone to part with their dollars, but if your donors are confident you and your organization will spend every dollar wisely to fulfill your mission, it will make the process much easier.

I remember when I took my first hourly job as a sales associate at Sears. Those first few months were nerve-racking. I was on my very best behavior. I didn't want to get fired from my first job and I knew they could let me go at any time if I wasn't a good fit. The company did a 3-month, 6-month, and a yearly review to ensure I was capable of doing the job they hired me to do.

Think about the thank-you plan as a review for your donors. They don't ask for a written report at the 3-, 6- or 12-month mark, but imagine if you went above and beyond to include details about how your organization is making a difference with stories and examples of the impact. Your donors would be blown away. Of course, they wouldn't have invested in your cause if they didn't believe you were capable of doing the job, but you want them to continue to give monthly or yearly. If you don't do what you said you'd do in Step 6 when you asked for their gift, they will eventually pull their support.

I encourage you to communicate along the way about your progress and the impact you are making so they understand and feel they're a part of the process. This goes back to inviting your donors to be insiders to your organization. Their donation means they want to be involved in the process and the progress. Don't be afraid of over-communicating. Imagine how you'd like your favorite charity to communicate with you, so do that for your donors.

TRACK YOUR DATA

As your organization and donor list grow, you'll start to realize that it is nearly impossible to track each relationship without the help of taking notes. If your organization is large enough you should have access to a database program that shows the details of each donation that is received by your organization.

Documenting the history of each donor is critical to your long-term success. It may seem like a lot of work now, but you and your organization will be thankful to have historical data as you grow and come across staff turnover.

As you know, death and life changes are inevitable. Not every marriage lasts and no one lives forever. The last thing you want to do is mail a letter or call and ask for a deceased member of the family. We're bound to make a mistake along the way, but if someone's address changes or they've changed jobs, you want to be sure you can update their information. Being able to document those changes will ensure you maintain relationships with your donors and you don't look like a fool or upset anyone by bringing up sensitive life changes.

After my father's passing, my mom received a number of calls and direct mail pieces from charitable organizations addressed to him. It took nearly a year after his passing to get the communication to stop or to remove his name. Can you imagine how upsetting that would be to continue to receive calls and mail after the loss of a loved one?

If you have a relationship with your donors, you would be aware of these important life changes and immediately make notes and edits to your database. Some individuals may request not to receive newsletters, letters, or phone calls, and you'll need to suppress them in your database. This is critical, not only because they made the request and you want to honor that, but it can also be against the law to continue to send communication if they've requested to be taken off your list.

The other important thing to note is that your donors will tell you a lot of valuable information about themselves if you pay attention. They will share how they want to be communicated with and what is important to them. If you don't take notes and just blanket out the same communication to everyone on your list, it shouldn't be a surprise that you lose donors throughout the years. They will start to feel like a number and that you have automated your communication.

Donors will be extremely loyal if you make it easy and show you care. Your donors will be proud to align with you and your organization if you do this step well. Your donors will become more committed to your cause and they will find that they can't help but tell others about the great work you are doing.

Pay attention to birthdays, anniversaries, hobbies, travel, and activities they enjoy. This information will help you as you send out gifts. It can also help as a conversation starter to build and grow your relationship. At the core of it all, we all want to be seen and appreciated. If you genuinely care about your donors, they will know it. Continue to reevaluate and meet with your donors to find out more about why they support your cause. Ask for their feedback on how you can improve your communication and continue to share important updates. If you listen and take action, they will notice.

GO CHANGE THE WORLD

"Without charities and nonprofits, America would simply not be able to operate." – Charity Navigator

Many claim that people are more self-centered than ever, yet donations and volunteering continue to increase. Studies show that when we make a charitable donation, parts of the brain that are associated with pleasure and reward light up in MRI scans. That's right, we all "want" to give because it feels good.

I believe that as humans we want to take care of each other, but it is up to us as nonprofit leaders to ensure that our donors have no question whether we are making an impact or not.

I hope these steps give you encouragement and clear direction that it is possible to achieve your fundraising goals. You are doing incredible work to change the world, and I encourage you to press on during the ups and downs of the job. There is a lot of work to be done and the world is counting on you, on charitable organizations, to make a difference.

Take a moment to go back to Step 1 and reflect on your vision. Your vision should be focused, with clarity, on what you are capable of accomplishing. You'll never be the answer to all of the world's problems, but you have a mission and a calling to make things better for a specific cause. Don't lose sight of the end goal as you walk through this process. It will sustain you during the tough times.

Go back to the picture you created in Step 1 and stay focused. No single gift should change the focus of your vision. Write down what is expected of you as a fundraiser and acknowledge your compensation. Sit back, be grateful, and enjoy the successes of the work you and your team have accomplished. Celebrate all that you have and will accomplish together, and don't take for granted all that you have been gifted to do.

I recall sitting at the dinner table with two of my first fundraising mentors. The two women were bouncing stories back and forth about their years in fundraising when the older of the two leaned over and said to me, "If you want to stay in this industry you must celebrate the successes. They don't come near enough."

That was nearly fifteen years ago but I hear that woman's voice every time I see a large donation come in. I sit back and take a deep breath, and say to myself, "Celebrate this success. It won't come again soon enough." I encourage you, as my mentor encouraged me, to celebrate. Take it all in and don't let those moments pass you by.

Reflect on the work you put into the process and remind yourself of all the hard days and the good days it took to get to this moment. Think about the difference this donation will make for your cause. Remind yourself why you were called to do the work you do and don't forget how fortunate you are to serve others. Every dollar you raise brings you closer to your vision.

Thank you for investing the time and energy to take the journey through the 7 Steps. I look forward to hearing about your journey and how these steps are impacting your work. Don't rush the process, but enjoy every moment of the journey.

Go change the world one volunteer
and one dollar at a time!

NOTES

Chapter 1

1. Purdy, J. (2012). 5 Things You May Not Know About the Men Who Built America. Retrieved from http://www.history.com/news/history-lists/5-things-you-may-not-know-about-the-men-who-built-america
2. Examples. Retrieved from https://topnonprofits.com/examples/
3. Get Giving USA. (2016). Retrieved from https://givingusa.org/see-the-numbers-giving-usa-2016-infographic/
4. Mail, B. Charity Navigator - Your Guide To Intelligent Giving. Retrieved from http://www.charitynavigator.org/index.cfm?bay=content.view

Chapter 2

1. Budget | National Institutes of Health (NIH). (2016). Retrieved from https://www.nih.gov/about-nih/what-we-do/budget
2. The Society is the largest voluntary health organization in the world with 96 percent brand recognition. (2016). ACS Cause Marketing.

Retrieved from http://www.cancer.org/aboutus/ honoringpeoplewhoaremakingadifference/ corporations/corporatealliances/acs-cause-marketing

3. What it Takes to Break World Records - Strengtheory. Retrieved from http://www.strengtheory.com/ what-it-takes- to-break-world-records/

4. Flandez, B. R. (2012). The Cost of High Turnover in Fundraising Jobs. Retrieved from https://www.philanthropy.com/article/ The-Cost-of-High-Turnover-in/226573

5. Your body language shapes who you are. (2012). Retrieved from https://www.ted.com/talks/ amy_cuddy_your_body_language_shapes_who_you_ are?language=en

6. Cuddy, A. J. 2015. Presence: Bringing your boldest self to your biggest challenges.

Chapter 3

1. New Cone Report Values America's 100 Leading Nonprofit Brands. (2009). Retrieved from http:// www.conecomm.com/news-blog/new-cone-report- values-americas-100-leading-nonprofit-brands

2. Sports Scout Career Information - IResearchNet. (2015). Retrieved from http://career.iresearchnet. com/career-information/sports-scout-career/

3. Ramsey, D. (2011). Entreleadership: 20 years of practical business wisdom from the trenches. New York: Howard Books.

4. What's next for Apple? Retrieved from http://www.cbsnews.com/ news/60-minutes-apple-tim-cook-charlie-rose/

Chapter 4

1. Howard Schultz. (2016). Retrieved from https://news. starbucks.com/leadership/howard-schultz

2. Company Timeline. (2016). Retrieved from https://news.starbucks.com/facts/company-timeline
3. Starbucks. Retrieved from https://en.wikipedia.org/wiki/Starbucks
4. Pitts, A. (2013). You Only Have 7 Seconds To Make A Strong First Impression. Retrieved from http://www.businessinsider.com/only-7-seconds-to-make-first-impression-2013-4
5. Design Shack - Web Design Gallery, Articles & Community. Retrieved from http://designshack.net/articles/inspiration/10-tips-for-designing-logos-that-dont-suck/
6. Why Do I Need a Website? Here are 21 Reasons. (2015). Retrieved from http://bigmouthmarketing.co/why-do-i-need-a-website/

Chapter 5

1. Volunteering in the United States, 2015. (2016). Retrieved from http://www.bls.gov/news.release/volun.nr0.htm

Chapter 6

1. Ramsey, D. Dave Ramsey's complete guide to money: The handbook of Financial Peace University.
2. Get Giving USA. (2016). Retrieved from https://givingusa.org/see-the-numbers-giving-usa-2016-infographic/
3. The Center on Philanthropy at Indiana University
4. U.S. Trust Study of High Net Worth Philanthropy. (2014).
5. Charitable Giving Statistics. Retrieved from https://www.nptrust.org/philanthropic-resources/charitable-giving-statistics/
6. Bank of America Study of High Net Worth Philanthropy. (2014).

Chapter 7

1. Chapman, G. D. (2005). The five love languages: How to express heartfelt commitment to your mate. Waterville, Me.: Thorndike Press.
2. (2012). Thanking Donors-Once is Never Enough. Retrieved from http://www.cdsfunds.com/thanking_donors_once_is_never_enough.html

ACKNOWLEDGMENTS

This book has been on my heart for many years, but I had no idea how hard the journey would be and how many people would be involved in the process. I couldn't possibly thank everyone who has touched this book, but I'll hit the highlights.

Special thanks to:

The 5 most influential people in my life – my husband, Geno; my mother-in-law, Karen; my spiritual mentor, Ginni; my dear friend, Kelli; and my author coach, Kary.

Kary Oberbrunner, my book team captain, for sharing your wisdom and platform to ensure my vision of becoming an author became a reality.

The Igniting Souls Tribe, my rock star team of author friends, for your daily encouragement and for the constant reminder that we are better together!

My incredible editor, Precy Larkins, and team of proofreaders who spent countless hours sharing their feedback and advice to ensure this was the best book it could be for the reader.

ABOUT THE AUTHOR

Former Development Director for the American Cancer Society, the ALS Association and Special Olympics, Mary Valloni has raised millions of dollars and spent countless hours in the field of development. In the process, she realized too many charities were being underfunded and missionaries were coming off the field due to their lack of training. Mary knew things had to change.

In 2014, she started Mary Valloni Consulting with the dream of spreading a message of hope and encouragement to nonprofit leaders and missionaries across the country as a fundraising coach, consultant, trainer and author.

Mary is a passionate and energetic speaker who is equally at home leading national nonprofit training sessions as she is speaking to college students and community volunteers. Mary works with international, national, and community-based organizations, individual fundraisers and missionaries to help them develop fundraising strategies to generate revenue so they can impact the world with their mission.

Mary received her Bachelor of Science in Organizational Communications with a minor in Religious Studies from Missouri State University and attended her first year of college in her home state at the University of North Dakota. Mary currently resides in St. Louis, Missouri with her husband, Geno, and their Dalmatians, Kota and Puck. To connect, visit MaryValloni.com.

FUNDRAISING FREEDOM COACHING COURSE

The fastest, most effective way to master
Mary Valloni's 7 Steps

Take action today and let Mary be your guide through a 7-week interactive video course. She will be your personal coach as you walk through the 7 steps to build and sustain your next campaign.

Through the Fundraising Freedom Coaching Course, Mary will show you how to:

1. **Focus Your Vision** with templates to create your mission, vision, timeline, and budget.

2. **Run Your Research** with downloadable spreadsheets and tips to find the "right" prospects.

3. **Enlist Your Team** with sample job descriptions to recruit your lead volunteer.

4. **Enhance Your Brand** with access to sample logos, one-pagers, case documents, and websites.

5. **Deploy Your Team** with team-building strategies and tips to running effective committee and leadership meetings.

6. **Organize Your Ask** with strategies and stories to ensure you are effective and dollars aren't left on the table.

7. **Make Your Difference** and ensure you celebrate your success and thank your team. Mary shares her top thank you ideas with you here!

To join the Fundraising Freedom Coaching Course
visit MaryValloni.com

Bring Mary Into Your Organization

Author. Trainer. Speaker.

Mary knows the importance of bringing in the right trainer and speaker for your team. Set the stage for success with an energetic, passionate fundraiser who can connect with your audience. Mary will customize each message and training to bring the content and motivation to equip your team to overcome obstacles and take action.